A CHOSEN BULLET

A BROKEN MAN'S TRIUMPH
THROUGH FAITH AND SPORTS

D1273313

BILL RENJE

GROWING UP AS A SPORTS FAN myself in Illinois, I can understand and easily relate to Bill's passion for Chicago sports teams. The valuable lessons he learned from the accomplishments and disappointments of these teams, the support he has gained from his family, and the transforming grace of God he embraced while attending our church, has enabled him to experience triumph in spite of the overwhelming obstacles he has faced. A Chosen Bullet will inspire readers to see that with God "all things work together for good ....".

—DR. KEN WHITTEN
Senior Pastor Idlewild Baptist Church in Tampa, Florida

"*A CHOSEN BULLET: A Broken Man's triumph through faith and sports* is the life story of one of the biggest Chicago Bears' fans ever. The impact of faith and sports on Bill's life will inspire and motivate you to believe in the power and grace of God. In 1985, the Bears captivated the nation by dominating on the field with focus and determination like no other team in NFL history. 25 years later I learned that our team also inspired one of our greatest fans to win and triumph in the biggest game of all - THE GAME OF LIFE. A triumph in which he has showcase in a must read. A Chosen Bullet will awaken the consciousness within your soul to God's unconditional love and grace."

—TYRONE KEYS
Super Bowl XX Champion & Founder of All Sports Community Service

A CHOSEN BULLET

A BROKEN MAN'S TRIUMPH
THROUGH FAITH AND SPORTS

BILL RENJE

A CHOSEN BULLET

A BROKEN MAN'S TRIUMPH THROUGH FAITH AND SPORTS

Printed in the United States of America

ISBN: 978-1-935507-45-1

Cover Design & Page Layout by David Siglin of A&E Media

AMBASSADOR INTERNATIONAL
Emerald House
427 Wade Hampton Blvd.
Greenville, SC 29609, USA
www.ambassador-international.com

AMBASSADOR BOOKS
The Mount
2 Woodstock Link
Belfast, BT6 8DD, Northern Ireland, UK
www.ambassador-international.com

The colophon is a trademark of Ambassador

For Nico, Noah and Dani Rae:
my three most precious gifts

"THE WORLD OF CHICAGO SPORTS has always been built on the principles of heart, toughness, grit and determination. Drawing from the lessons taught by Windy City giants like Ditka, Payton and Jordan, Bill Renje Jr. tells us how he rode his own remarkable perseverance on his way to writing an admirable tale of personal redemption and triumph."

—KEVIN KADUK

Editor of Yahoo! Sports' Big League Stew and author of Wrigleyville

"BILL'S JOURNEY TOLD IN THESE PAGES is inspiring. His spirit comes alive as a great example of courage and will to his children and family. It's a lesson every kid in the Chicago schools should hear -- not to mention every Chicago sports fan who shares his passion."

—DAVID HAUGH

Award-winning sports columnist with the Chicago Tribune

TABLE OF CONTENTS

INTRODUCTION

My first sports memory occurred on December 18, 1977. I was six years old, had just awoken from a nap, and came downstairs to find my dad watching the end of the Bears-Giants game on a cold, frozen field in the Meadowlands. To this moment, my sole memory of that day is the white road uniforms of the Bears moving in tandem with a snowy, gray, and icy backdrop. Those white uniforms exuded sure jubilation the same way we did as kids when we got really excited about a new toy or going to an amusement park. That was the moment Bob Thomas kicked the last-second, game-winning field goal on the final game of the regular season to give the Bears a 12–9 victory and send them to their first playoff appearance since winning the NFL Title in 1963. Never mind that the Bears would get drubbed 37–7 the following week by the eventual champion Dallas Cowboys. That was the moment I became hooked as a Chicago sports fan. It was the moment a passion was born that has not subsided in the ensuing thirty-three years.

A Chosen Bullet is the story of what my passion as a Chicago fan has taught me in life and the struggles this passion has helped me to overcome from the day a 9mm bullet ripped through my neck from five feet away My life has been contrasted by deep darkness and then glorious light, characterized by overcoming through perseverance, stained by first underachieving and then finally experiencing success that few will ever know. With the support of my family and eventually my deep-abiding Christian faith providing my foundation, these values and lessons intertwined with my thirty-three year journey as a Chicago fan to take me from tragedy to triumph. All the while, my lifelong experiences of rooting for the teams of my youth and studying my hometown heroes has helped mold and shape me to become the person I am today: from a permanently paralyzed victim of a gunshot to a very happily married man, a blessed father of three children, a successful businessman, and a two-time Paralympic gold medalist.

Chicago is the greatest sports city in the world. It's a city where sporting traditions, stories and love of the city's teams go back over a century and have been handed down to four different generations. I remember the roar at the Chicago Stadium and the smells, sights, and sounds of the old Comiskey Park. Long before everybody else was doing it, I remember the exploding scoreboards, fog horns after goals, spotlight introductions, and Gary Glitter's "Rock and Roll Part 2." I was there on the floor, ten feet from the court, during the deciding Game 6 of the 1992 NBA Finals.

Being a Chicago fan includes all the elements of real life: exhilaration but more often frustration, victory but more often defeat, triumph but too often tragedy. Being a Chicago fan has taught me all about being accountable, overcoming adversity through hard work and struggle, and seizing the moment, as well as the pitfalls of resting on your laurels and underachieving, along with combating unfilled potential. We too often focus on the negative in sports and, to be sure, there's no shortage to the dark side of athletics. *A Chosen*

Bullet, however, is a story about life lessons learned and teachable moments as told from my life's perspective about the men and teams I've watched, studied, and emulated throughout my life and the influence they've had on me.

SECTION I

Rock Bottom

Please God—don't let me go out like this. The thought raced through my head as I feared death while gasping for air. A bullet from a 9mm gun had just ripped through my neck, severing my spinal cord and deflating my right lung before finding its final resting place. This is where my story begins—the early morning hours of June 17, 1989.

A friend of mine and I had left a party to pick up some drugs on a well-known drug corner on 135th Street, south of Kedzie in Robbins, Illinois. We noticed a drug raid underway as we pulled into the lot with me driving. In a scene that could have appeared on the TV show *COPS*, we saw guys we assumed to be drug dealers lined up facedown on the ground with their hands behind their heads. Jail not seeming like a very good option, my buddy nervously said "Get out of here" and I agreed. And then, out of the shadows, came a plain-clothes, undercover police officer. On foot, he approached the driver's side of my car with his gun drawn, telling me in no uncertain terms to get out of the car. As I drove past him, ignoring his order, I heard the sound of a loud firecracker going off, only it wasn't a firecracker but a gunshot, and in an instant my life changed forever. The driver's side window shattered and a split second later my body went numb—everything seemed to silently go into slow motion as I knew in that moment I was paralyzed. I moved my arm to reassure myself that my arms still worked, but the rest of my body felt frozen.

As I regained my breath in the ambulance, I realized I wasn't going to die. I allowed myself to drift in and out of consciousness and eventually fell asleep. In the emergency room, the nurse told me that they were going to call my parents. "Please don't," I begged them. The last thing I wanted was for my mom and dad to be awoken in the middle of the night by that dreaded call. Seemingly only seconds later, they arrived. There lay their firstborn son—broken, paralyzed, beaten down, and at what truly was "rock bottom."

Over the course of the next few days in intensive care, all I had was time to think how much I had underachieved up to this stage of my young life. I had just graduated high school yet lacked direction with a focus largely on going from one party to the next. I started smoking pot recreationally as a freshman in high school and had long since graduated to harder as well as more dangerous drugs. Now, almost a month shy of my eighteenth birthday, I was a failure, an underachiever, left with the "what ifs" and the "would've, should've, could've" just like so many of those teams I followed growing up.

CHAPTER 1

Blue Heaven Lost

C hicago always has and always will be a Bears town. Other teams may rent that space from the Bears for a period of time like the Bulls in the '90s or the Cubs or Sox in various one-off years of success, but we'll always be a Bears town. In the early '80s, in an otherwise dark era of Chicago sports, the DePaul Blue Demons rented that space and pretty much took over the city's sporting conscience. This was pre-Jordan and if you offered a fan a ticket to either head out to the Rosemont Horizon to watch DePaul or to the Stadium to watch the Bulls, well, suffice it to say that fan would've been headed out to Rosemont.

I was ten years old in 1981 when I started following college basketball. DePaul had been to the Final Four in '79, losing by two points to Larry Bird and Indiana State. In 1980, they were the consensus top-ranked team from early January on and entered the NCAA Tournament as the overwhelming number one seed. And then they promptly went out and lost 77–71 to UCLA, the eighth seed, in their first game (note: the top four seeds in each region received byes until 1985 when the tournament went from forty-eight to sixty-four teams). That loss provided a premonition of colossal failures and letdowns that dogged the last five years of Ray Meyer's otherwise great coaching career and in my mind marks a stretch of unfulfilled potential that I've not seen in my lifetime of watching college hoops, or any other sport for that matter.

The year 1981 was supposed to be payback time. DePaul entered the season even stronger with a couple of local stars: junior forward Mark Aguirre, the best player in the country and future number one overall NBA draft pick, as well as sophomore Terry Cummings, who would be the number two overall pick the year after Aguirre. Cummings would go on to win the NBA Rookie of the Year, and both players experienced All Star–laden pro careers. So the 1980–81 DePaul Blue Demons were absolutely loaded. All of Chicago was captivated as was the entire country as it seemed Dick Enberg, Al McGuire, and NBC were in town every Saturday afternoon to nationally broadcast the Blue Demon game, which was a big deal before cable TV took off and became what it is today.

They rolled through the regular season going 27–1 including a revenge 93–77 thrashing of UCLA in late December. Again they entered the tournament as the overwhelming top seed and again they would fail, but this time in the most horrific of ways. Playing the number nine seed, Saint Joseph's (PA) out of the Atlantic 10 should've been a tune-up to bigger and better things, and apparently the players felt the same way as they were lulled into a low-scoring, defensive slog fest.

What I remember most was DePaul's panicked final possessions and missed foul shots (they weren't "free" throws to those DePaul teams) down the stretch including a 1 and 1 by Skip Dillard that could've sealed it with thirteen seconds to go. Instead of clinching the win, Dillard, nicknamed "Money" for his 85% free throw shooting, missed his foul shot. At that point sheer panic set in which led to an open layup at the buzzer by John Smith of St. Joe's, and just like that—game over, season over. Mark Aguire screamed in agony as he cradled the basketball, squeezing the life out of it. The Blue Demons just simply quit after the missed free throw as St. Joe's raced down the court. On the final layup, St. Joe's had three players in the paint, near the basket, and undefended without a Blue Demon in sight. Mental toughness—a trait needed to be a champion—simply eluded this and other DePaul teams, and thus they fell well short of their goals despite their immense talent levels. This was my first taste of what it felt like as a Chicago fan, in those years, to feel absolutely sick to my stomach. I remember just walking around my neighborhood in disbelief afterward on what otherwise was a beautiful March day. I didn't even know where St. Joe's was located and they had just beaten my mighty team. I learned that in a split second, all your hopes and dreams can be ruined if you don't seize the moment, if you don't take advantage of your opportunities while you have them.

Again in '82, DePaul went into the NCAA Tournament as a number one seed and again, for the third year in a row, they lost their first game. It's hard to believe, and even today as I write this it is no less painful. In '84, Ray Meyer announced that he'd be retiring at the end of the season and everyone was hopeful for a John Wooden or Al McGuire-type ending culminating with the Blue Demons' cutting down the nets in their coach's final game. There was hope after they actually won their opening game to advance to the Sweet 16. But once again, they couldn't handle the pressure of the number one seed and quit, this time blowing an eight-point lead to Wake Forest before eventually losing in overtime. Wake Forest sent the game to overtime with a buzzer beater and ended the game—and Ray Meyer's career—with a basket as time expired. Talk about a double whammy! As a fan, the sick feeling from these losses never goes away, even after twenty-five years, but they do provide teaching moments and examples to learn from of the emotional and mental toughness it takes to be a winner in life. DePaul had a couple more seasons of success with Joey Meyer leading Rod Strickland and Dallas Comegys before the program slipped into irrelevancy by the early 1990s. I often wonder how the fortunes and future of that program might have been different if not for the five-year stretch of falling woefully short of their talent and abilities. That '80–'81 squad provided their best opportunity; Ray Meyer's best opportunity and the end result was unfulfilled potential. I want to add, because it's a lesson learned, that I met "Coach Ray" in 1985 in the parking lot of the Rosemont Horizon after watching DePaul beat Marquette. He was retired for a year and leaving to go home with his wife, Marge. I remember how unassuming and humble this man was despite, at the time, being third on the all-time wins list. He very graciously signed an autograph for me, and when I asked him if he thought "we'd go all the way," he said, "Yes, I think this could be the year." I learned from Coach Ray how to stay grounded and to appreciate common people like me.

CHAPTER 2

1984

Raised in the southwest suburbs of Chicago, first in Country Club Hills and then in Tinley Park, I first and foremost was a White Sox fan when it came to baseball. But I wasn't an either/or as in "Sox or Cubs." I always considered myself a Chicago fan, meaning I rooted for the teams with Chicago on the front of their jerseys. I played all sports that were in season. But baseball was my sport. I spent the first twelve summers of my life (before I discovered girls) eating, sleeping, thinking about, and playing baseball. I'd get up in the morning, play until one o'clock, come home, and watch the Cubs. I'd hang out, figuratively, in the living room with Jack Brickhouse on channel 9 during the afternoon, go back out and play ball until dinner time, and then come in and spend my evenings with Harry Caray and Jimmy Piersall on channel 44 while watching the Sox games.

Neither team was very good when I started following baseball in 1978 and not much changed over the next five years. But something was special about Major League Baseball. I played organized baseball all throughout grade school, and to think that grownups could put on big league uniforms and play in big league parks on TV and get paid well for it—wow, that was cool! All I ever wanted to be growing up was a baseball player. So I watched, listened, and studied their every move. I hung on to every word Jimmy Piersall said when he would start out a sentence with "for you youngsters watching at home …" in describing how a fielder made a play. Through baseball and taking countless groundballs from my dad and playing catch in the front yard, I first learned the art of practice and repetition in perfecting my potential. Baseball is a sport in which things seemingly go wrong for no apparent reason. You can be hot with the bat and unstoppable as a pitcher; then, without doing anything differently, you can go into a hitting slump or stop throwing strikes as a pitcher. It's a game that teaches you to constantly work on perfecting yourself as a player—when something goes wrong, you try to figure out how to adapt and fix it. But it's also a game, more so than any other, where you need to keep your composure. During a 162-game season (twice as long as any other sport), you can't get too high with the highs or low with the lows. Years later as a quadriplegic, these lessons came roaring back to me. Being paralyzed from the chest down without function of ninety percent of my body forced me to adapt, adjust, and figure out through problem solving as well as trial and error how to survive.

By 1983, Chicago put together a two-year stretch of winning baseball. I'll get back to the '83 "winning ugly" White Sox later; but 1984 was the year that I learned what it was like to be a Cub fan. I had heard all the stories from my aunts, uncles, and grandma about the heartbreak of 1969 and I was about to experience that firsthand myself. The '84 Cubs had all the elements that came to describe a classic Chicago sports tragedy. Not much was expected of this club in spring training.

I remember *Sports Illustrated* picked them to finish last. But general manager Dallas Green made move after move in putting together an instant contender. What I remember most about that summer was just how alive Wrigley Field became. This was long before Wrigley became a tourist destination, known now as the World's Largest Beer Garden, where sellouts are almost guaranteed. I also remember how larger than life Harry Caray became that summer. Although I loved listening to Harry when he was with the Sox, whom he left for the Cubs in 1982, this was the first time I heard him broadcast a winner. And as the summer went on, the more animated Harry became. The Cubs were on WGN, by then a super station, and Harry seemed to know that the entire country was tuning in to watch the Cubs. Keep in mind as well that this was pre-stroke Harry who, while maybe not completely in his prime, was clear and crisp nonetheless. As opposed to the lovable grandfather figure that he became in his final years, Harry was still on top of his game. This was the Harry that helped teach me to be passionate and love what you do. He truly believed as he once proclaimed at the end of a "thrilling victory" that "God wants the Cubs to win!"

For a while, it did seem like God was a Cub fan, but no one could imagine at the time just how bad it would all come crashing down. After winning the division, the Cubs played San Diego in the Best of Five National League Championship Series for a chance to go to their first World Series since 1945. In March of '84, I had been through the last of the DePaul disappointments. And I had heard all about curses, black cats, and ghosts as well in 1969. So I wasn't naïve about what may have awaited that

October. But it's safe to say that after the Cubs held off the Mets (their '69 nemesis) to win the division and throttle the Padres 13–0 and 4–2 in Games 1 and 2, I felt a rematch of the '45 Series with the Tigers was in the works.

The Cubs headed out to Southern California needing one victory in three attempts over a team they had just dominated in Wrigley. I still felt confident even after a Game 3 loss and Game 4 when the Padres' Steve Garvey belted his opposite field game winner in the bottom of the ninth off Lee Smith, as right fielder Henry Cotto tried in vain to keep the ball in the park. On a side note, I met Garvey in a memorabilia shop in 2007 at Ceasar's Palace in Vegas. When I told him that he broke our hearts in '84 he joked that he still needs to bring extra security with him when he travels to Chicago. I met Pete Rose the next day at the same shop, and Rose, when told I'm from Chicago, quipped that when he retired from the game he wanted to get as far away from Major League Baseball as possible so he "rented an apartment on Waveland Avenue [the street Wrigley Field is on]." The lovable loser jokes are endless.

But back to the '84 NLCS, which was now tied 2–2. Cub fans felt good because we had Rick Studcliffe (that's right, I spelled it with a *Stud* instead of a *Sut*). Sutcliffe was as close to automatic as any pitcher I'd ever seen either before or since that summer. Since coming over in the Carter/Hall trade, Sutcliffe went 16–1 with a 2.69 ERA. The guy was absolutely incredible and won Game 1 13–0. So mythical, he hit a homerun in that game. (In a twist of irony befitting of Cubdom, the only NL pitcher since to hit a homerun in the NLCS was Kerry Wood in 2003 [Game 7] when the Cubs were also only needing one victory in the final three games of the NLCS to get to the World Series.) So, no, I wasn't overly concerned and became less so after the Cubs took a 3–0 lead after the second inning. Sutcliffe mowed the Padres down for five shutout innings. It really looked as if "next year had arrived," and then it all came apart.

The Padres scored two to cut it to 3–2 in the sixth and the cloak of invincibility on Sutcliffe started to fall off. With one out and a runner on second, pinch hitter Tim Flannery hit a hot smash, albeit routine groundball, right at Leon Durham. If Durham fields it cleanly, there are two outs with a runner on third and Sutcliffe likely pitches his way out of the inning. But we all know what happened—the ball went between Durham's legs, tying the game. Three successive hits later, the score was 6–3; Sutcliffe, the heart and soul of the team, was done and so were the Cubs. The headline in the *Chicago Sun-Times* read "Paradise Lost" the next day as the Cubs failed to get that final win as San Diego stole the Cubs' ticket to Detroit.

So what lessons did I learn from the '84 Cubs? Like with the DePaul debacles, I learned that you had better take advantage of your opportunities when they come around because there are no guarantees that you'll get a second shot. And for that '84 Cub team, there would be no second opportunity. Although they started off strong in '85 and were in first place in mid June, they soon suffered a thirteen-game losing streak from which they would never recover. By July, their entire starting rotation was on the disabled list (only with the Cubs is this possible), and they finished the season 23.5 games behind St. Louis.

I also learned from their General Manager Dallas Green about setting lofty goals, having a vision as well as a plan, and ultimately seeing through its implementation. While the '84 Cubs stared down their demons and their past by making it to the postseason for the first time in thirty-nine years, it was those same demons that they succumbed to in not fulfilling their potential. In a scene that would play out again almost twenty years later in 2003, it was not bad luck but rather a self-fulfilling prophecy of inevitable failure once something bad happens—the feeling of "oh no, here we go again" that's reinforced by history every time one puts on a Cub jersey or reads a newspaper or watches ESPN. It's a self-fulfilling prophecy that the organization still has not been able to overcome all these years later. Resiliency, toughness, persistence, perseverance, and ultimately overcoming all odds are the traits of champions—in sports, in business, in families—and they are traits that the Cub organization has never been able to develop.

SECTION II

The Struggle (1989–1991)

Four days after my injury, I was moved from the Intensive Care Unit of Northwestern Memorial to the spinal-cord injury floor. I lay there paralyzed and weak—unable to do a single thing for myself: unable to eat, bathe, dress, sit up in bed, or even roll over on my own. I couldn't even blow my own nose. Broken physically, mentally, and emotionally, I lay there in my own private pit of misery from which there looked as if there'd be no return. My parents, brothers, grandpa, grandma, aunt, and uncle were there in the room in those early days. I had let them all down. *How could all of this happen?* I thought. The answer basically was that I was not emotionally, mentally, or spiritually tough as an adolescent. Simply put, illicit drugs, as well as alcohol when abused, are for weak-minded people—regardless of one's circumstances or background—of which I was one.

Although not a spiritual person at the time (that would come a few years later), I did have a sense that the Lord allowed this to happen. I would realize years later that it was God who allowed me to be broken down so He could build me back up again. And He would use sports as an important vehicle to accomplish this task. I failed to live up to the kind of person my parents raised me to be in adolescence. I was the oldest of three sons, and my brothers, Dave (three years younger) and Steve (seven years younger), and I enjoyed an unassuming upbringing—meaning it was relatively normal. We went to church, although there was minimal spiritual emphasis growing up. My mom was a fulltime homemaker although she had the occasional part-time job. Her day started early, around 7:00 a.m., and consisted of getting my brothers and me off to school, then doing laundry, housekeeping, and errand-running until we came home from school. Then she piled us in the car and we were off to either Cub Scouts, baseball practice, or some other activity before she made dinner and cleaned up. If there was any time left in the evening after baths, she used it to go grocery shopping or prepare for the next day. My mom went like clockwork from 7:00 a.m.–10:00 p.m. seven days a week.

My dad was as routine as they come and about as predictable as the sun rising and setting every day. The man got up every morning at 6:00 a.m., was off to work by 6:15 to his job as a computer technician (the same job he'd have for forty years), came home around 4:30 or so, and then either coached baseball for one of us or worked around the yard until it was time to sit on the couch around eight o'clock or so to enjoy a ballgame or one of his favorite TV programs, usually a crime show like Quincy or the Rockford Files. In the twenty years I lived under his roof, the man never took a sick day and never complained about being sick or complained about anything, for that matter.

Predictability is a good thing, leading to comfort and security, which is important to the upbringing of a child. And my pre-teen childhood is one full of happy memories, warm summer days, playing ball, riding bikes, making forts in the woods, and having snowball fights in the winter with other kids like Wayne Sone, Kevin Gleich, and Billy Rapka, as well as Karen and Gary Thorne. I learned to play baseball with Kevin and Billy as we played in our yards as well as on a tee ball team coached by my dad and Kevin's father. Growing up in the 1970s and early '80s, we were the last of the "outdoor generation." We bought our first video game system (Atari) in 1981 when I was ten, and cable was installed in '83 with a home computer to follow in 1985. Don't get me wrong; I'm all for technology. But my childhood provided a time when I'd do anything to get out of the house because no reason existed to stay inside. But even more so, my generation was the last where parents could allow their kids to wander around the neighborhood all day, ride bikes, and play in the woods until sundown without fear that one of us may end up on the back of a milk carton. I embraced being an outdoor kid, and sports provided a backdrop and foundation for most all of my outdoor activities. Even on rainy days, baseball provided a focal point for us as young boys. Some of my fondest memories were of sitting around on my bed with two or three friends and our shoeboxes full of baseball cards. Studying our favorite player's statistics on the back of the cards, we'd wheel and deal in making trades while learning the art of negotiating and compromising at an early age. Those days of kids bartering over trading cards and the lessons learned from that kind of group interaction are gone forever in the video game generation.

I also enjoyed a close-knit extended family with both sets of grandparents as well as aunts, uncles, and cousins within a thirty-minute drive. Both my parents grew up in strong traditional families. My grandfathers were strong-willed figures who got up every day to provide for their families, and the main priority for both of my grandmothers was to care for their husbands as well as their children. Those values and ethics filtered down the family tree. A game always illuminated the TV at any family gathering, as sports truly were the "ties that bind" in my family. I couldn't talk about world events, work, or politics with my uncles, but I could freely engage and hold my own when it came to discussing the problems plaguing the Cubs, Sox, or Bears. The wonderful thing about a solid foundation is that while some kids may veer from the values of their upbringing during their teenage years as they struggle to form their own identity, most will return if they don't die along the way. This theme certainly plays out in my life story. So in a setting such as this, the question became how and where it all went wrong for me.

In a nutshell, I started going down the wrong road in junior high when I began paying more attention to my peers and less attention to my parents. I took them for granted and assumed they were supposed to love and care for me because that was their parental responsibility. In a sense, I thought they were just doing their job, so I sought value in people who didn't have to like me. I cared way more than I should about what my friends thought, and that's dangerous at any stage of life but certainly more so in your formative years. I became a follower as opposed to a leader. At the same time, I did have the "party gene." It was a gene that passed over both my parents who were about as straight-laced as they came but a gene nonetheless that was on both sides of the family as evidenced by various aunts, uncles, cousins, and second cousins. A follower who has the party gene is a lethal combination.

I remember during 7th grade playing in a wooded area near my house with a friend of mine when an older kid showed up with a pack of cigarettes wearing an Ozzy Osbourne shirt. I still remember looking at that Marlboro box, hearing my mom's voice in my head, and getting out of there as fast as I could. Two years later, I became that kid.

A little light bulb went off inside of me in eighth grade that said "become a rebel," "eat from the forbidden fruit," and "do everything the opposite of what your parents and authority figures are telling you to do." And guess what—I did just that as I started experimenting occasionally with pot, cigarettes, and alcohol toward the end of eighth grade and on into my freshman year of high school. Still, my partying was minimal as I maintained my participation in sports. I wrestled my freshman year, but my real focus was on making the baseball team. My freshman class at Victor J. Andrew was loaded with baseball talent. By my senior year, that core of players took our school to the state semi-finals: as far as our school had ever been in football, basketball, or baseball. We had more than eighty players trying out for a twenty-man roster, and it's safe to say we really had sixty-five guys trying out for five spots as twelve to fifteen were locks to make the team. Nonetheless, I played with confidence; baseball was my sport. I played organized ball from first through eighth grade, usually batting leadoff or second while playing second base. I routinely made the traveling All Star teams and, while I was lacking confidence at that point in most areas of my life, I was confident in my abilities as a ball player.

I don't remember much about the week-long tryout other than not doing a great deal to distinguish myself from the other players trying out. I made the first two cuts and, the morning after the last tryout, I went to check the list only to not find my name on it—that was it; I was cut and my dream died. Looking back, I should've used that motivation to work harder, play in a summer league, and come back stronger the next year. The coaches offered a second tryout over spring break for guys to come back out who thought they deserved a second look. But I didn't take advantage of this opportunity. I gave in to excuses, finger pointing, and blaming others. It was the coaches' fault because they picked favorites. They overlooked me because of "politics," which is what everybody who is bitter says when something doesn't go their way and they don't get what they want. Either way, I was done with baseball and done with organized sports in general. I had been "cut" and wasn't good enough at the only thing I felt good at. From there, I drifted down to the lowest common denominator: the stoner crowd, known then as "metal heads" for their love of heavy metal music. I was now a follower without any goals or ambition and, with the party gene, a lethal, toxic combination with the potential for disastrous results.

Over the summer after my freshman year of high school, my party lifestyle started to pick up, mostly with marijuana and hanging out at the park smoking cigarettes. They teach in early grade school that "you are what you eat." What they should also teach is that "you are who you hang out with." For me, most of the kids that I played ball with around the neighborhood growing up were now in the party phase of their lives. To be sure, I made my own decisions, and not all the kids from the neighborhood went down the path I did; but I gravitated toward those that were in that bottom rung—classic underachievers without direction other than focusing on the next party. In June of '86 I was fourteen and remember vividly when I found out that number two overall NBA draft pick Len Bias died of a massive heart attack brought on by cocaine use. I told a friend who wasn't going down the same route as me that I would *never* do cocaine, and my friend replied, "That's what you said a year ago about marijuana."

"No, you don't understand," I replied. "I will never do cocaine."

When it comes to drugs, addiction is a very gradual yet slippery slope. Nobody becomes a hardcore meth head or crack addict overnight. They start slowly, usually with marijuana, maybe monthly, then weekly, then daily. Eventually, a need develops to graduate to higher highs (which subsequently have lower lows). That's my story. I went from occasional pot smoker my freshman year of high school to a full-fledged coke addict by the end of my senior year. My first experience with cocaine (the drug I would "never do") happened toward the end of my junior year. Simply put, five or six of us were in an apartment and everybody was snorting coke. Although scared to death, I was such a follower that when the straw and mirror were passed to me, I snorted my line. With an incredible rush, I thought it was the greatest feeling in the world. There seemed to be no lingering effects of withdrawal or wanting more, and it took very little (maybe an inch-long line) to achieve euphoria. At that point, I thought cocaine was a safe, harmless drug that certainly didn't live up to the hype of the "anti-drug crowd."

Well, let's just say that the devil is very cunning; he draws you in as your friend and then proceeds to very subtly and very gradually rip out your soul. And that's what cocaine is—a white devil on a mirror. The first few times I did coke it took very little to achieve the high I was looking for, and the withdrawals were minimal to non-existent. But the more you do, the more it takes to achieve the same high, with the withdrawals and cravings becoming much more intense and severe. Eventually, my use escalated to the point of weekend addiction. I remained functional, meaning I held down a part-time job working in the hardware department at Sears my senior year. I went to school and graduated on schedule, which is more than I can say for most of my friends who either dropped out or were kicked out. But my life started coming apart at the seams toward the end of my senior year. I started selling other drugs and scalped tickets to get cash to buy my coke. About a month before high school graduation, I was introduced to crack cocaine, which took my addiction to an even higher level. Hooked the first time I smoked it, I used it a few times a week until that fateful day of June 17, 1989, when a divine appointment with a bullet promptly ended the drug phase of my life.

CHAPTER 3

The Boys of Summer

As Chicago sports were a part of my fabric and very being, so too would they become part of my recovery. The summer of 1989 wasn't exactly how I visualized my summer after high school graduation; but again, I began to see a larger, more divine purpose for my life even if I didn't completely recognize it at first. I did realize that my drug days were over, that I easily could've been killed and now had a second opportunity to make the most out of my life—which one doesn't always receive. While in the hospital, I learned that I would never walk again. Of course, at that time I denied this reality like everybody else who suffers a severe spinal cord injury. Think about it: I was eighteen and now being told that I'd have to spend the rest of my life in a wheelchair. *No way; that doctor doesn't know what he's talking about,* I thought. *I'm walking outta here or they're gonna take me out in a body bag.* Here I sit now, twenty years later, and I remember a guy coming to visit me who had been in a chair for ten years. I thought to myself then that there's no way I could imagine living in a wheelchair for ten years; I'd rather be dead.

After about three weeks at Northwestern Memorial, they transferred me across the street to the Rehabilitation Institute of Chicago (RIC) to begin the long and grueling road of physical, occupational, and emotional therapy to try to become a productive, albeit disabled, member of society. In a lot of ways, I was blessed, again, even if I didn't recognize it at the time. RIC exemplified a state of the art facility with a world-class reputation. And I had a support system, chiefly my parents and brothers, who rallied around me. Neither one of my parents, although I'm sure they thought it, ever gave me a guilt trip about "being a bad kid" or "not appreciating or listening to them" or "how much of a disappointment I was" and, truth be told, they had every right to do that as I failed to live up to the standards and expectations of how I was raised. But my parents gave me exactly what I needed at the time with unconditional love and support. They drove the forty-five minutes one-way almost every day from our suburban home to RIC, which is located downtown. I met a lot of other guys in my predicament whose family and parents weren't around to support them. At that time, I realized the fallacy of what I believed as an adolescent, now understanding that my parents made a conscious choice to love me and, for that, I found fulfillment in their support. I very much saw the parable of the prodigal son as told in the Gospel of Luke played out by the grace, love, support, and forgiveness shown to me by my mom and dad.

All that said, I truly lay at rock bottom, physically. I had no strength and wasn't even able to sit propped up in bed at a forty-five-degree angle for more than fifteen minutes without passing out. Early on, maybe the first day or two, a therapist laid out for me that eventually, with extreme hard work and effort, I'd be able to live an independent life—meaning I'd be able to dress, bathe, take care of myself, drive a car, and have sex (very important for an eighteen-year-old male). That was pretty much the time I realized I'd be okay, even if I didn't walk again. *I'll manage,* I thought, *as long as I don't need to rely on anybody to take care of me.* They explained to me that I was a "C6-7" quadriplegic, meaning my injury level was at the sixth and seventh cervical vertebrae located at the base of the neck. I had impairment in all four limbs, which categorized me as a "quad," meaning four, as opposed to a "para," meaning two. (Paraplegic injuries are primarily the result of back injuries while quadriplegics are primarily the result of neck injuries.) And the higher up on the spinal cord the injury, the less the function. Paralyzed from the chest down, I would be able to regain enough upper body strength and mobility to lead a relatively normal life. My right side would be stronger than my left side with normal triceps muscles and some finger mobility in my right hand, and weaker triceps and no finger movement in my left hand—all of which was a blessing because I am right-handed.

Still, a long haul awaited me. I was like a baby, having to learn how to do everything, *everything*, all over again—brushing my teeth, feeding myself, dressing, and bathing. Unlike a baby though, I knew what I wanted and needed to do, but my body was unable to respond as the messages from my brain couldn't make their way down my irreparably damaged spinal cord. All tasks were like mountain climbing as my body's physical strength had dwindled to almost nothing. Frustration definitely set in at times, especially when my therapist came into my room first thing in the morning wanting me to practice dressing myself. I hated dressing because in the beginning it took me forty-five minutes to put on a pair of sweatpants and, believe it or not, that so fatigued me that I just wanted to go back to bed. But, like doing the same, monotonous drills such as taking groundballs in the front yard over and over again, it became gradually easier, and by the time I left RIC three months later, I cut that time down from 45 to 5 minutes. Repetition and consistency were traits learned from watching my dad do the same things over and over again while having the same daily routine. Those traits would serve me well over the years in honing my skills first as a student, then as an athlete, Christian, husband, businessman, and finally as a father.

Even as daunting as the physical aspect of the rehabilitation was, the psychological and emotional recovery would be one hundred times more difficult. Rehab truly was an hour to hour, day to day recovery. There's no looking and planning even a day down the road, let alone a week or a month. Gone was any thought of looking forward to a future. How could I think of a future involving school or work or family when I couldn't even sit upright at a ninety-degree angle without passing out, couldn't push a wheelchair across the room, couldn't get out of bed to get into the wheelchair, and couldn't get dressed to get out of bed? These were the dark times—an eighteen-year-old broken down in every way, now having to rebuild himself not only physically but emotionally and mentally as well.

That said, rehab in and of itself wasn't too bad in providing comfort to me because everybody was either like me or understood me. My home for the summer of '89 was the seventh floor—the spinal-cord injury floor. The summer months are when the majority of injuries take place, the most common among them being car accidents, diving, and, in a city like Chicago, gun shots.

Young males ages eighteen to twenty-four are the predominant demographic that suffer spinal cord injuries because of the inherent risk-taking in that group. I spent the summer in a four-bed room and the guy next to me was a nineteen-year-old named Mike Rembis. Mike broke his neck playing hockey at the University of Illinois and arrived at RIC a week before me, and we were side by side all summer. We quickly became pretty good friends, and he was the first friend I had made in a long time that actually had a good head on his shoulders in terms of ambition and direction. Through his influence, I eventually would decide to challenge myself at a university like Illinois. I also had an entire floor of peers from every walk of life: rich, poor, suburban, inner city, black, white, and Hispanic who all shared a common bond and plight. RIC was staffed with doctors, nurses, physical and occupational therapists, social workers, as well as psychologists, all of whom had an intimate understanding of what I was going through. No more pretending to be someone I'm not—I'm a quad, a cripple, a gimp—we all were at RIC. In short, it was the opposite of what it would be "on the outside."

My first experience of life on the outside happened a month into my four-month rehab stint. My dad pushed my wheelchair two blocks away from RIC to Lake Shore Drive to watch the annual air and water show taking place over Lake Michigan. It was a gorgeous summer afternoon with a gentle breeze blowing in off the lake. As we sat there for a few minutes, however, I began to look around and felt thousands of eyeballs looking at me as if I was the show—a sideshow, a circus act, a freak. I felt like a stranger in a strange land and immediately ordered my dad to take me back to rehab where I would feel secure in my own bubble, which I never wanted to leave again.

Back at rehab, I started to embrace, if not cherish, my daily routine, which started around seven o'clock when the doctor with his full entourage of interns and students showed up in my room to poke and prod me both physically and mentally. After the nurse helped get me up and dressed, it was off to the common area on the floor for breakfast at eight, then a combination of physical, occupational, and psychological therapy from nine to twelve, lunch, then more afternoon therapy before dinner. Evenings were usually spent lying in bed recuperating for the next day while socializing with my three other roommates, family, and the occasional visiting friends.

Among family and friends, and deep dish pizza from Gino's East, I celebrated my eighteenth birthday in rehab on July 26, 1989. Not the ideal birthday party but nonetheless one in which I realized how blessed I was to have the unconditional love of my parents, brothers, grandparents, aunts, uncles, and cousins. There were some guys, especially those from poorer backgrounds, who had few if any visitors and little support from their family. It was my parents who began to go through and contact the dozens of names and numbers given to them by the floor social worker to line up services for me that I'd need once I returned home. Those services ranged from wheelchair-accessible transportation services to get me back and forth to school as well as outpatient therapy, home modification sources, and, most importantly, funding sources, as my dad's insurance covered only four weeks of rehabilitation when I needed sixteen weeks. For a while there was talk of my parents having to take out a home equity line. After probably hundreds of calls, we received aid from the state, although I eventually would have to pay back the aid. I know I took years off my parent's lives that summer and, although I didn't realize it at the time, my family had to go through all the mental and emotional adjustments I was going through and would continue to go through for the next couple of years. I realized then for the first time that a family is like a team, and when one goes through a crisis as well as a subsequent recovery, the other members go through it.

At this point, a month into rehab, I started gaining enough strength from therapy to push my wheelchair, slowly at first and not very far, but what a huge early success! I also began to try to sit up and transfer myself from the bed or therapy mat into the wheelchair, although always with a therapist spotting me. And at this point Chicago sports, in particular baseball, would once again play a prominent role in my life.

After getting cut from my high school baseball team as a freshman, I severed ties from the sport that was the first love of my youth. For the remainder of my high school years, I spent most of my summer nights partying while the Cubs and White Sox spent most of their nights floundering at or near the bottom of their respective divisions. Like in '84, the 1989 Cubs weren't supposed to do much, and, like in '84, the 1989 Cubs became the talk of the town during the summer—

including throughout the Rehabilitation Institute of Chicago where I had taken up residence for the summer and was about to rediscover my first love.

Only a few holdovers remained from the '84 squad, chiefly among them perennial All-Star second baseman Ryne Sandberg and Rick Sutcliffe, who, while not as spectacular as in his career year in 1984, still held the distinction of veteran anchor of the pitching staff. The staff was led that year by Greg Maddox who, at twenty-three, came of age in the second full year of what would be a Hall of Fame career. Another cornerstone was Andre Dawson, now in his third year and two seasons removed from being the only MVP of a last place team for the cellar-dweller Cubs of 1987. So the Cubs had established talent in place although nobody expected them to challenge the Mets or Cardinals, who ruled the National League East for each of the previous four years.

What set those Cubs apart, however, were guys who never played as well before or after 1989. Mike Bielecki went 18–7 as the number three starter behind Maddox and Sutcliffe. Les Lancaster had a 1.36 ERA out of the bullpen, and the lineup got a jolt from center fielder Jerome Walton, who hit leadoff, as well as left fielder Dwight Smith—they finished first and second respectively in the 1989 Rookie of the Year balloting.

More importantly to me, the '89 Cubs provided an outlet, a source of entertainment at an otherwise miserable time of my life. I honestly don't know if I would have made it through that summer without the day in, day out excitement and adrenalin the Cubbies gave me. Most of the staff at RIC lived on the north side and they loved the Cubs, so there was a constant source of conversation other than disability-related concerns and issues. Even though they installed lights at Wrigley the year before, the Cubs played mostly day baseball, and a TV always sat nearby tuned into a Cub game, whether on the therapy floor or the common area on the seventh floor. I vividly remember the afternoon of Tuesday, August 29 when, with a 2.5 game lead in the division, they fell behind Houston 9–0 in the fifth inning before storming back and eventually winning 10–9 in the tenth. Everything seemingly stopped that afternoon at RIC as we all cheered as if we were an extension of the Wrigley Field bleachers in watching such an incredible comeback.

In early September, part of my therapy plan was to go on outings around the community, in part to get acclimated to venturing outside the walls of RIC. For me, this exercise was exciting but terrifying at the same time since my anxiety attack at the air and water show a month before. I had not left my comfort zone since that gruesome experience and now was tasked with not only leaving my comfort zone but planning the outing as well as part of the therapy. Three of us were in my group with two therapists. Each of the three patients chose and then planned an outing. One guy wanted to go to the top of the Sears Tower, one wanted to go to the airport to get a tour on how someone in a wheelchair could maneuver through an airport and board a plane, and I chose to go to a Cub's game. Going to Wrigley to watch the first-place Cubs in the heat of a pennant race on a beautiful September afternoon provided the exact therapy I needed to get over the anxiety I felt over not fitting into society as someone with a disability. We pushed through the crowds, sat in the bleachers above the famous ivy-covered wall, ate hot dogs, jeered the opposing outfielders, and cheered the Cubs.

Though a few months passed before I completely became comfortable with fitting back into society, going to Wrigley that day was the first step in the process for me. After holding off both the Cardinals and Mets to win the division, the Cubs lost the National League Championship Series to the superior San Francisco Giants. But I'll always hold the '89 Cubs in high regard for helping me get through the toughest summer of my life. They taught me that sports is a healthy outlet, as opposed to my previous self-destructive outlets, in getting away for a few hours from the harsh riggers and reality of life.

In late October after four months of grueling rehabilitation, the time came to go home. Although cheered by those around as a time of accomplishment and excitement, fear and panic simultaneously gripped me. I left my comfort zone, a place where everyone was like me or understood me, to enter into a new "real world" as a young man stuck in a wheelchair where it seemed nobody was like me.

CHAPTER 4

Winning Ugly

I arrived home in late October of 1989 to a far different world than I had left just four months before. After growing up as a white male, I was now a "minority"—a "person with a disability" and a member of the most traditionally disenfranchised group in society. My self-esteem, while slightly higher than in rehab, still resided at ground zero levels. My physical recovery, also on the rise, had a ways to go. I relied heavily on assistance from my parents when it came to everything from going to the bathroom to dressing and bathing.

My parents' home, a tri-level with a sub-basement, was not wheelchair accessible and would not be for several more months. With the exception of going down to rehab a couple of times a week for outpatient therapy and the occasional trip to the mall, I spent most of the next couple of months isolating myself at home, watching sports and movies. Most of my so-called friends dwindled away slowly after my injury, and that wasn't necessarily a bad thing. My dad kept harping on me during high school to not be so concerned about pleasing my friends or being a part of the crowd. He used to say that "ten years from now, you're not going to know where most of these people are at and you're not going to care." Of course he was right, although I shunned his advice at the time.

At one point, I realized that there had to be something more in life for me. I couldn't sit around the house for the rest of my life, dependent on my parents and brothers. One snowy day in early December, I looked outside my parents' house and thought how much I loved the snow and playing snow sports. But those days were over as wheelchairs and snow, or ice, do not mix. For the first time, I envisioned moving to a warm climate someday but understood I needed to chart a different destiny first. I picked up the phone and called the vocational rehabilitation therapist from RIC. She was as surprised as anybody would be to hear from me, as I had ignored her during my rehab stay to the point of being rude. The purpose of Vocational Rehab (VR) is to assist and prepare people like myself with educational training as well as job opportunities to plug back into society as a functional member. As stated previously, the difficulty for me was to think a day or week in advance while in the fog of emotional recovery. So when the VR counselor came to see me to discuss long-term goals like school and work, I quickly shut her down, often times acting abrasive and cold.

By this time, however, I realized I needed to start thinking about my future. I had never been a good student, simply because I didn't apply myself in high school. I always thought I would end up doing something "blue collar." But now I knew I couldn't use my hands to make a living so I needed to figure out how to use my mind. I met with the VR counselor and began to map out a plan for my future. Around this time, all my therapy began to pay off as I gained more and more independence when it came to my daily life skills. I learned how to transfer myself in and out of a car by using a transfer or sliding board with one end on the seat of the car and the other wedged between my butt and my wheelchair. I then started venturing out more, mostly with my three closest friends, Rob Carlson, Derek Svehla, and Justin Damm who had stuck by me through the entire excruciating experience. Slowly but surely, six months after my injury, things started to fall into place. My life and what I had to go through may not be pretty; in fact, it may be ugly at times, but nonetheless a determination and resiliency began to grow inside of me.

Every child has a favorite memory or memories of places they visited during childhood. For some, that place may be as simple as a tree house or an ice cream stand. For others, it may be Disneyworld or an amusement park. For me, that place was the Old Comiskey Park located on the corner of 35th and Shields on the Southside of Chicago. My grade school gave out free tickets for every quarter semester in which you had perfect attendance. I prided myself in early childhood for not missing school for any reason so I could get my hands on those tickets. And inevitably every summer, my dad and I went to three or four White Sox games free of admission. I have fond memories of going to Disneyworld when I was five and seeing Cinderella's castle, and I remember the feeling of adrenalin when my family made our annual summer trip to Six Flags Great America and you could see the roller coasters from the car as you neared the park.

But nothing for me can top seeing the lights atop Comiskey as we approached the park traveling northbound on the Dan

Ryan Expressway. I strained with anticipation and asked my dad "where is it, where is it, where is it?" and then I'd see it to the left hovering above the other nearby buildings. I remember the lively scene as we exited the off ramp and saw the crowd and cars being drawn into "The Baseball Palace of the World" as if being pulled in by a tractor beam, the street vendors and parking lot attendants all part of the scene. And then, as I stepped out of the car, there it was, so big; the park was larger than life. I handed my ticket to the usher and went through the turnstile. Once there, all the aromas of the park hit me in perfect unison—the popcorn, the peanuts roasting, and, of course, the hot dogs. I couldn't wait to sink my teeth into a ballpark hot dog. To this day, I've had hot dogs at all sorts of different venues, picnics, and events. But I've never tasted a better dog than one at a ballgame.

As my dad held my hand, we made our way underneath the concourse to our section. I remember walking and waiting for the section number to line up with our ticket number. My heart beat through my chest as my anticipation grew. And once we found our section, the walk up the stairs toward the light of the park was glorious. Arriving at the top of the tunnel, the most incredible scene I could ever witness as a little boy awaited us—a big, beautiful park with more than 40,000 green seats, a huge scoreboard that set off fireworks after a homerun (the first of its kind), a beautiful, manicured lawn with the lines going the same way as opposed to that of my little league field, and a real, elevated dirt mound which was the centerpiece of the infield. After we found our seats, I'd wander around the park to take it in from every conceivable angle. Once the game started,

I sat there with my fielder's glove on, never knowing when a foul ball might find its way to me. And once my brothers were old enough to join my dad and me, I would be their tour guide around the park: "There's the shower in the centerfield bleachers where you can cool off on a hot summer day," "Look, there's Harry and Jimmy in the booth," and "There's Nancy Faust in the organ loft." We always arrived early enough to enjoy batting practice and I was able to study my favorite players and analyze their batting stances and fielding techniques. To this day, there's not much better than the sound of the crack of the bat and the ball hitting the mitt—both of which instantly take me back to warm memories and the innocence of childhood. Looking back, Comiskey Park was really a dump when compared to the newer parks of the modern era. But like an old mitt or hat, I enjoyed familiarity with that park. I'll never forget the old plumbing fixtures, the mile-long horse trough urinals in the smelly bathrooms, and so many coats of semi-gloss paint over those bricks. I cried when the Sox played their last game there in 1990 and again over that winter when the wrecking ball hit for the first time as a part of my youth was being torn down.

The Sox weren't very good those first few years, and I remember asking my dad why they always seemed to lose when we went to a game. As a matter of fact, I think we probably attended a dozen or so games over the course of three or four years before they finally won. But all that changed by 1983. While Sox owner Bill Veeck innovated making the ballpark experience a memorable one for me as a youth, he didn't do much to improve the team on the field. While commonplace today, Veeck first made going to a ballgame an experience when it came to the exploding score board, the centerfield shower, ball day, hat day, and having Harry Caray sing "Take Me Out to the Ball Game" during the seventh inning stretch. Unfortunately, he bought the Sox during the advent of free agency and just couldn't afford to field a very competitive team. The Sox of the late '70s were led by the likes of Chet Lemon, Lamar Johnson, and Jorge Orta—not exactly household names.

When Veeck sold the Sox after the 1980 season to an ownership group led by the then unknown Jerry Reinsdorf, the stage was set for the glorious summer of 1983. The new ownership's first move was to sign All Star quality players and name brands like Greg Luzinski and the best catcher in baseball, Carlton Fisk. The new player acquisitions were no small feat given the anemic Chicago sports landscape at a time when it came to star-studded teams. In the first four years I followed the Sox, they were never a threat and finished an average of seventeen games out of first place each year. By 1982, they were within 2.5 games of first place in mid August, finishing the season only six games in back of the division-winning California Angels.

Expectations were high headed into 1983. Besides Fisk and Luzinski, they had young players coming into their own like Harold Baines and '83 Rookie of the Year Ron Kittle. A young manager named Tony Larussa looked to get his first taste of the postseason with this club. The season started inconspicuously enough as the Sox found themselves seven out of first place in early June. By the All-Star break, they climbed to third place, three games behind the Texas Rangers. To commemorate the fiftieth anniversary of the All-Star game, Major League Baseball awarded the game to Comiskey

Park, where the inaugural event was held in 1933. On a glorious July night, the American League battered the National League 13–3, winning the mid-summer classic for the first time in eleven years and, incredibly, only the second time in twenty-one years.

Whatever winning aura took root that night in the winner's clubhouse apparently stuck around because the White Sox were about to go on a run for the ages. The Sox went 59–26 after the All-Star break, including an incredible 29–6 record to close the season. They took over first place on July 25 and never looked back. The thing is, these Sox were anything but remarkable. They weren't particularly flashy and, if anything, could be a bit mundane in the way they won. The Sox used hustle and played a scrappy brand of ball, which nonetheless was effective. Texas Ranger manager Doug Radar, whose club the Sox would bypass for first in the standings, claimed the Sox were "winning ugly" and their success would not last. What Radar didn't know was that not only would the Sox success continue, he had just given the Sox marketing department a catch phrase that would take root, define this team, and give a fan like me a perspective that I'd use later in life.

The city of Chicago, so desperate for a winner in a town mostly void of contenders of any sort since the '63 NFL champion Bears, began to catch the fever in late July. My entire family (mom, dad, both brothers, and I) went to Comiskey Park on Labor Day and watched the Sox drub the A's 11–1. That was the first time that I had gone to watch a winner in person. All those games I watched an inferior team, and now I enjoyed taking in my team as a winner, in the park I loved. I still have the foul ball I fielded during batting practice for the A's. I sat along the short fence, maybe three feet high, along the left field line almost to the base of the outfield wall when future Hall of Famer Rickey Henderson hit a grounder that somehow eluded two dozen or so other nets and gloves. My new souvenir found its way into my glove as I briefly jumped onto the dirt warning track to field the ball before quickly disappearing back into the stands. For over five years I had brought my glove to the ballpark and now I had something to show for it. Twenty-seven years later, the ball with the autograph I got from Tony Larussa that day as he signed alongside the Sox dugout sits on my memorabilia shelf. I tried the same trick two years later, with the ball in my glove and both feet firmly planted in the same spot down the left field line, when Kansas City pitcher Bud Black spotted me. Black, warming up in the outfield, yelled at me with all the grace of a drill sergeant, telling me starkly to get off the field. Completely scared, I threw the ball back, jumped over the fence, and sprinted as fast as I could back to my seat. Not too surprisingly, the take-charge Black is now the manager of the San Diego Padres.

On Saturday, September 17, VCRs were set all over Chicago, for those who owned them, and when Harold Baines's sacrifice fly in the bottom of the ninth drove in Julio Cruz with the winning run, the city had its first winner of any kind in twenty years. The franchise that finished an average of almost twenty games out for the first four years that I followed them now finished in first— twenty games over the second-place Royals.

Expectations ran extremely high going into the Best of Five American League Championship Series against the Baltimore Orioles and were even more so after Lamar Hoyt shut down the O's for a 2–1 victory in Game 1. Although the Sox lost Game 2, they returned to Chicago where the final three games of the series would be played. With two more victories, the Sox would be in their first World Series since 1959. They lost Game 3 11–1; but if they could just win Game 4, I thought at the time, we'd have Hoyt on the hill in Game 5 and no team could beat him. But, like so many other sporting disappointments in my childhood, I learned the art of handling disappointment and patience as I'd wait another twenty-two years to see a World Series in Chicago. Even though Sox pitcher Britt Burns threw masterfully, the Sox bats tightened up in the clutch and, despite ten hits, they were unable to plate a run through nine innings.

For fans with long memories like me, we'll never understand what Jerry Dybzinski was thinking in the bottom of the seventh inning. In what would be the Sox's best opportunity, they led off with back to back singles. With Dybzinski now up, he failed to bunt the runners over to second and third. With a force out at third, the Sox now had runners on first and second with one out. Julio Cruz, the scrappiest of all the Sox, brought the already roaring crowd to another level with a sharp single between short and third. Third base coach Jim Leyland held up the runner Vance Law at third, but instead of bases loaded, one out with leadoff hitter Rudy Law and his team leading .389 series average coming up, Dybzinski suffered the brain lapse of all brain lapses. One of the first things they teach you, from the time you're six years old is, as a base runner, *do not* look at the ball; rather look at your base coach. So what does Dybzinski do? He got caught up in the moment, not to mention a rundown, as he never looked at Leyland. And thus, he rounded second and headed for third not realizing that Law had stopped at third. With the ensuing rundown, Law took off for home and was thrown out by a mile—all of which effectively killed the rally and sucked the air out of the park.

The Sox never scored, and without a true closer all year, Larussa sent Burns and his 136 pitches out to the mound for the tenth in a scoreless game. After getting one out and nearing 150 pitches (this was before the obsession with pitch counts), Tito Landrum sent a low line drive through the wind into the leftfield seats. I knew the game and season were over, even before the O's tacked on two more runs as the Sox's and the city's hopes ended in a 3–0 defeat. Like so many other Chicago baseball teams in my lifetime, the '83 Sox never came close to duplicating that success again. In hindsight, the Orioles were just a much better team with three future Hall of Famers. The Sox, in contrast, were gamers who worked hard and went the unconventional, if not ugly, way to success. If only for one season, they were able to maximize and get the most out of their talent.

One of the major turning points in my post-injury recovery occurred when I enrolled at Moraine Valley Community College, located twenty minutes from my parents' home, in January of 1990. Like I said, I had never been a serious student. But now, I was six months post-injury and looked forward to the challenge of being successful academically. I knew no other option existed. If I failed as a student, the reality that stared me in the face was a life of living with my parents and drawing a $500 monthly disability check.

Without an education, what else was there for me to do? Still doing outpatient therapy twice a week, I decided to start off slow and took two classes (six credit hours): a 100-level English as well as a psychology course. A funny thing happened: with a non-polluted mind, I discovered that I actually enjoyed learning and liked the idea of pushing myself to get good grades. Of course, I needed good grades, as I wanted to transfer to a four-year university after receiving my Associates Degree. My high school transcripts were insufficient (1.8 GPA on a 4.0 scale). But a second opportunity presented itself and one I took full advantage of—with sixty hours from an accredited junior college, a university would not require an ACT or SAT or look at my high school transcripts.

With a fresh start and a new-found spark of ambition, I became determined to be successful in the academic side of my college years. At the time, I had yet to learn how to drive with hand controls, let alone get a wheelchair in and out of the car. So I relied on a disability-equipped public transportation van to get me back and forth to school, the same service that took me to and from rehab for my outpatient therapy. Although somewhat humbling, the service nevertheless provided me with a means to get back and forth. I immersed myself in my studies that first semester and received an A and a B, which was no small feat considering that my high school transcripts were loaded with Cs, Ds, and an occasional F. I now had the confidence to enroll fulltime with fifteen credit hours the following fall.

Along the way, an even larger factor worked in my life. I learned through going to junior college that I wasn't a leper and possessed the capability of making friends. Many of my high school peers attended Moraine and most, if not all, treated me with the same respect and dignity as if I were able-bodied. At the same time, I made a lot of new friends and enjoyed relationships that I hadn't thought possible just a few months before when I viewed rehab as my safe zone.

I hooked up with my buddy Tony Granata in junior college, with sports again playing a vital role in my recovery. Tony would pick me up and take me to parties or we'd go out to watch Hawk games as well as go to Cub games. Most people thought it would be tough to go out to crowded places like a baseball stadium. Tony, for his part, would say he would just get behind and let me lead the way, as I always cleared the path of people afraid of being run over by a wheelchair. Once seated in the park, all are equal as fans as disability ceases to exist in the single pursuit of cheering for one's team. The first able-bodied friend I made after my injury, Tony told me years later that the reason he hung out with me was not because he felt sorry for me but rather because we'd always have a good time. So from both an academic and socialization aspect, I view taking the small yet big step of going back to school as a vital part in my overall recovery.

Now one year post-injury, I completed my outpatient therapy, could take care of myself independently, and looked forward to learning how to drive a car. The driver's education facility was located in South Bend, Indiana, which is where I spent one week alone in an apartment the facility provided for me. So not only would I learn to drive there, I'd be staying by myself for a week where all the tools of independence that I had worked on and used over the past year in both inpatient and outpatient rehab would be put to the test.

While I proved to myself throughout the week that I could live and function independently, driving for the first time with hand controls gave me a whole different perspective. For one thing, when you're out on the road, you're on par with everyone else. Everyone driving a car is your equal—nobody is more or less "able" than anybody else. The freedom of driving brought a tremendous amount of liberation, as I loved being out on the open road. In some ways, I found it easier to learn how to drive with hand controls. As opposed to using two pedals, you have a lever bar underneath the turn signal. The bar is connected to the brake and gas; you push down toward the floor for the gas and in toward the dashboard for the brake. I think I was on the road with the instructor for a grand total of fifteen minutes before being completely comfortable and at ease with driving a hand-controlled vehicle. I felt good at the end of the week as my parents drove me home, knowing that a little over a year earlier I couldn't even prop myself up in bed, and now I'd be able to live on my own, one hundred percent independent, as well as drive a vehicle.

At this point, the question became what kind of vehicle I would drive. A lot of people were steering me toward a van, telling me I couldn't drive a car simply because I couldn't get my wheelchair in and out of the car. *Nonsense*, I thought. *I'm going to drive a car.* And this was the first time the inner trait kicked in of stubbornly willing myself to accomplish a feat that others told me was out of reach—it was the beginning of a theme that would play out repeatedly with me over the next twenty years as my sporting mindset kicked in fulltime, never to shut off again.

So the thought never entered my mind that I couldn't drive a car. I also knew that I'd figure out how to disassemble my wheelchair to get it into my car while learning how to reassemble it to get out. The question was only what kind of car I would drive. I needed a two-door car, big enough to lug my chair in with me. With $3000 to my name, I set out to find the ideal used vehicle, and when I found a tan 1983 Monte Carlo with 70,000 miles sitting on a lot near my home, I found the car I wanted. Of all the cars I've owned since, including a 2000 Monte Carlo SS and a 2005 Jaguar, my original Monte is the vehicle that I hold closest to my heart.

I can remember in the beginning the extreme degree of difficulty of getting my chair into the car. Like the first time after my injury I tried putting on a pair of sweatpants, it took me nearly half an hour to get my chair in the car. On a few occasions, I'd fall out of the car as I tried to lift my chair through the door. But like with the lesson of putting my sweatpants on or taking hundreds of groundballs in the front yard as a youth, I eventually perfected my craft after dozens and then hundreds of attempts, whittling that time down over the period of a few months to about five minutes from the time I unlocked my door to the time I drove off.

At that point, there was going to be no stopping me from accomplishing whatever I wanted to accomplish. Pulling an almost A-average as a fulltime student, I drove on my own (no longer relying on friends, family, and special services), ventured out like a normal nineteen-year-old, dated for the first time since my injury, and was about to discover a sport that would propel me to levels unthinkable at the time.

SECTION III

The Preparation (1992–1995)

I n the fall of 1991, I decided to give the sport of wheelchair rugby, a shot. The best way for anyone to learn about the game—the competitiveness, its rules, and some of its history—is to watch the movie *Murderball*. But, in short, the game is a sport played four on four indoors on a basketball court and incorporates rules from basketball, hockey, and soccer. The wheelchairs are custom-designed, evolving rapidly over the years with angled high-pressure wheels for speed and front ends built for high-impact blocking, hitting, and picking (holding an opponent's chair). A goal line eight meters wide sits on each end of the court, separated by orange cones. The object is to cross the line with two wheels and possession of the ball while the defense tries to keep you from scoring within the allotted forty-second goal clock similar to a shot clock in basketball. Typical games range in scores from the mid 30s to low 50s with one point per goal and four eight-minute quarters. The United States Quad Rugby Association includes 30 or so teams and has existed since the mid 1980s while the sport is played all over the world, enjoying status as a Paralympic sport since 1996.

Each player is given a classification based on their level of disability. The more function, the higher classification based on the following scale: .5, 1, 1.5, 2, 2.5, 3, and 3.5. The classes of .5s and 1.0s, having the least function, are strictly blockers while 3s and 3.5s are strictly ball handlers. Each team is capped at having eight points on the floor at a time. So you can have any combination of 8 points or less (4 players on the court). Based on my level of disability, I played as a 1.5 and was a cross between a blocker and a ball handler much like a tight end in football.

I first heard about rugby in 1989 when I saw a poster while waiting for the same elevator everyday that would take me to therapy during my rehab stint. My first thought in looking at the poster was *how in the world do quadriplegics (with limited upper body function) play rugby?* At the time, I was unable to push my chair more than five feet, with a nurse pushing me from my room to the elevator and handing me off to the elevator operator who then took me from my floor up to physical therapy where my therapist wheeled me into the therapy room. Skeptical of playing "disabled" sports, my second thought with regards to rugby centered on the sport as a lame attempt to get quadriplegics like myself involved in a recreational activity. But I eventually met a few of the Chicago players through hanging around rehab and more or less decided to join the team so they'd stop bugging me to come out. Let me tell you, from the get go I realized how wrong my "rec league" first impression of the game was and just how fast and competitive the sport proved to be. I also realized right away how hard I'd have to work to ever see the light of day as far as playing time.

We had fourteen guys on our Chicago team during my rookie season of 1991–92, and I sat a distant thirteenth on the depth chart—and bench—on a below average team. I endured a really difficult time that year just making it up and down the court in practice, often getting winded after a couple of possessions. My chair skills and thus my on-court maneuverability, as well as my all-around ball handling, were limited going up against guys disabled longer with more experience in handling their chairs. I spent a lot of time getting knocked out of my chair, and I was a turnover waiting to happen by either making a bad throw or dropping a pass. So, for me, my rookie year proved to be an eye opener of just how far I needed to go and just how hard I needed to work during the off season. Most of what I learned that first year was off the court and just as valuable as anything I ever learned on the court. Here I was twenty years old, going to junior college, and living with my parents. For the first time, I surrounded myself with teammates: guys who were ten, fifteen, and twenty years older than me who were married with kids, owned their own homes, and worked fulltime. At twenty years old, that was truly the first moment I realized I could live a full, productive life. For me, this was as important as any of the accolades that would come later from the sport.

As sport historically has been an area on the forefront of promoting race relations, our Chicago team truly personified a melting pot with a blend of inner-city and suburban players. Tuesday night practices were held in the city to accommodate the "city guys" while our Saturday practices took place in the suburbs to accommodate the "suburban guys." I know of no other segment of society outside of the military battlefield more color blind than a sports team. My formative years growing up in an upper middle-class suburb like Tinley Park afforded me very little interaction with non-whites. That said, I truly believe my sports background and love for my Chicago teams and players helped me to overcome stigmas about "blacks" at an early age. My childhood hero was Walter Payton and I never cared that the Bears had a black quarterback like Vince Evans—a rarity back then. I only cared whether or not he could help the Bears win.

My high school was ninety-six percent Caucasian and the surrounding town reflected this statistic. So my rookie year of rugby was a good experience for me. The two guys that first befriended me when doing outpatient therapy at RIC and then recruited me to play rugby were Andre Davis, a black guy, and Adrian Inguinez, a Hispanic guy. In addition to our common bond of being quadriplegics, our bonds as fellow athletes and teammates went well beyond our racial make-up and socioeconomic backgrounds. Traveling and rooming together on the road also provided us with opportunities to really get to know each other as people and for me personally to see the world through their eyes and experiences.

Our first road trip that season was a two-hour drive south to the University of Illinois. I had not been away from home since my injury and, at that time, I felt like a world traveler to spend a three-day weekend 120 miles from home. I also fell in love with the U of I campus. In my mind, this was where all the "smart people" went to school, as the best and brightest from my high school enrolled there. I realized, at that point, that I wanted to fully challenge myself academically by going to U of I. When I approached my Voc Rehab counselor with this idea, he tried to steer me to Southern Illinois University, where he thought the academics would be less challenging. But I refused to let him sway me; if I was going to do something, I would not settle for mediocrity. I wanted to be part of the best and continued to use naysayers to motivate me by putting a chip on my shoulder in developing a mental edge to drive me to success.

CHAPTER 5

Chip on the Shoulder

The phrase "a chip on one's shoulder" originated with the nineteenth century U.S. practice of getting ready for a fight by carrying a chip of wood on one's shoulder, daring others to knock it off. In all my years of following sports, I've never known anybody better at carrying a chip on his shoulder than Mike Ditka, whose Bears teams took on that same mindset. I remember before the 1985 NFL season being amused by a cartoon in one of the Chicago newspapers that showed a Bear player with big shoulder pads having a hard time getting through a door, with the caption reading "It must be hard getting around with such a huge chip on your shoulder." When the Bears have been at their best, and they were arguably the best ever in '85, they've done so with tenacity, grit, and a "chip on their shoulder" mentality engrained in their DNA from their founder George Halas. Halas, a Ditka mentor, coached him when the Bears won the NFL Championship in 1963—Chicago's last sports title heading into the 1985 season.

The '85 Bears took their cues from three people: Mike Ditka, Buddy Ryan, and Walter Payton. All three were limited somewhat when it came to natural abilities but nevertheless succeeded with a mental approach and level that few others ever reached. A desire burned deep within these men to overcome, often by using naysayers to put that chip on their shoulders. I first fell in love with and followed the Bears beginning in 1977, and Buddy Ryan had been their defensive coordinator most of that time. Ryan could care less what others thought about him and, much like Ditka, committed himself to channeling his tenacity and edge into success.

Although the defense played tough and rugged like their coordinator, the Bears overall were very mediocre in the late '70s and early '80s. They possessed a limited offense with anonymous names (save one), while built solely around Payton with the game plan usually "Walter to the right, Walter to the left, and Walter up the middle." All these years later and with all the football I've watched, I've grown even more appreciative of just how special a player Walter was and what a gift he provided me to be able to follow and learn from him. In my lifetime, there's never been more of a void of star quality players in the Chicago sports scene as existed in the late '70s and early '80s. Growing up a Chicago sports fan in this era, Walter was all we had, and a city priding itself on hard work, overachievement, and effort embraced Walter. Like Ditka, Payton embodied the "Chicago Tough" mindset.

By 1982, everything began to change for the better when Halas, in his last big moves before his death in '83, decided to retain Ryan as the defensive coordinator while hiring Ditka as the head coach. Almost instantly Ditka changed the losing mindset and culture of the Bears. He re-infused the Bear tenacity and aggressiveness that had been largely missing since he left as a player in the mid '60s. He promised Halas he was going to win a Super Bowl, which was a pretty lofty goal considering the team had only two playoff appearances and zero post-season victories in the previous seventeen seasons before his arrival. Ditka was so intense that he broke his hand when he punched a locker after a loss during his first season as coach. After a docile outsider like the previous coach Neil Armstrong, Chicago embraced Ditka with open arms. Even though he didn't grow up in Chicago, he was one of our own, having played the best years of his Hall of Fame career as a tight end with the Bears. As a player, there was no sophisticated formula to his style of play; he played and believed that you run straight ahead as hard as you can, as fast as you can, and either he was going to run you over or you were going to run him over. His nickname was Iron Mike, and he brought that same mentality with him back to Chicago as a coach.

Ditka obviously loved the idea of being able to build an offense around Payton, who in many ways embodied the same traits as Ditka (traits I've grown to admire in trying to emulate). "Da Coach," as he came to be known, was a no-nonsense, mind over matter, sheer will kind of guy. He really believed in a lot of ways that you could just impose your will, regardless of talent level, to overpower an opponent. So fiercely loyal, he embraced those who were hard workers and overachievers with a strong, disciplined mindset. He wasn't flashy and didn't give in or put up with excuses, cry babies, or losers. Ditka was all Chicago and never would have become what he became in some place like L.A., San Diego, or Miami—which is why he continues to be embraced and loved in the Windy City all these years later.

For his part, Payton was never the fastest back in the league or the flashiest runner. But his durability set him apart, and he is considered as possibly the best all-around football player of all-time when you combine the skill sets of blocking, receiving, and passing. To this day, he remains the Bears' career leading receiver in catches. In a lot of ways, watching Payton spoiled me as a kid in much the same way I would later be spoiled by watching Michael Jordan. With Payton, as later with Jordan, the extreme level of hard work and consistency set him apart from everybody else. I just assumed every week that Payton would carry the ball twenty times, rush for 120 yards, and score either a rushing or receiving touchdown. The amazing thing about Payton was his durability to keep getting back up as he mirrored a real-life Rocky Balboa, especially for the first seven or eight years of his career where defenses ganged up on him, knowing he was the Bears' only viable offensive threat. The guy only missed one game in thirteen seasons, playing on hard, artificial turf, no less. With all the NFL and team records he held at the time of his retirement, the most amazing feat to me was that he didn't have an All-Pro offensive lineman blocking in front of him until 1985—11 years into his career!

With guys embodying the Ditka/Ryan mentality like Payton already in place, the Bears drafted five future All-Pros, Ditka's first three drafts completed the nucleus to try to make good on his promise to Halas to win a Super Bowl—a vow he now promised to keep posthumously after Papa Bear's death on Halloween 1983. The Bears finished the '83 season a very respectable 8–8 after winning five out of their last six. A bit of foreshadowing took place as to how good the defense would become with a 13–3 smash mouth victory over the 49ers at Soldier Field on November 27. The 49ers were one year removed from winning their first of four Super Bowls in the 1980s. That win, in which the Bears sacked QB Joe Montana five times and intercepted him twice, provided the first statement game for what became arguably the best defense in NFL history.

Going into the 1984 season, the Bears were widely viewed as the favorites to win the NFC Central for the first time since league realignment created the division in 1967. On October 7, Walter Payton stepped into the history books by becoming the NFL's all time leading rusher by breaking Jim Brown's yardage record, a record largely accepted as the most cherished in professional football and along the lines of the homerun record in baseball. For me looking back, the record validated what can be accomplished with single-minded determination and toughness. Here was my childhood sporting hero, a guy from a small town who went to a small college, a guy who was not the biggest, nor the fastest, nor sleekest, nor most powerful runner, a guy surrounded for most of his career with average talent, but nonetheless a guy still considered as one of the best football players of all time.

As an adult, I've studied Payton both on and off the field. On the court of play, I've always tried to maximize my abilities and push myself beyond what has been expected of me. Off the field, I've tried to be the best person, husband, and father in going beyond my natural limitations. I remember one game that Payton almost missed because of a leg injury caused from stumbling down his stairs trying to keep his infant son from falling. That example of selflessness in a time where so many athletes now routinely, and without thought, are not around for children they father out of wedlock is one for all of us as men to heed. Here's a guy that by all accounts was a solid citizen, a strong father, as well as a good husband, and I'm convinced his character is a result of what he saw modeled in his home by his parents growing up in Mississippi.

The 1984 Bears got off to a fast start and were 6–3 when the defending Super Bowl champion Los Angeles Raiders came to town on an overcast November afternoon. The Raiders of those days with their "The quarterback must go down and he must go down hard" mantra were everything that Ditka, Ryan, and the Bears wanted to become. Those Raiders lived up to their name as well as their silver and black colors. They came to ravage, pillage, and plunder their opponents and weren't concerned with looking pretty in accomplishing their goals. That November afternoon became a statement game of sorts for the Bears. The rest of the NFL also went on alert that the Bears were on the prowl again. That game provided the coming out party for the famed '46 Defense—an innovative defensive scheme created by Ryan and named after hard-hitting former Bear Doug Plank who wore #46.

The Raider game was the most violent, intense game I've ever seen. Both starting quarterbacks left the game with injuries resulting from ferocious hits. Jim McMahon suffered a career-threatening lacerated kidney, of all things. He knew his season was over after the hit when, barely able to breath and helped to the locker room, he proceeded to urinate blood. Buddy Ryan had the Bears' defense amped up as well, as they knocked Raider starter Marc Wilson out of the game before knocking back-up David Humm out in agony. For a while, it looked like the Raiders would need to bring punter Ray Guy into the game to play QB as he warmed up on the sidelines. But Marc Wilson returned only to suffer another injury, this time to his knee, basically finishing the game on one leg. All told, the Bears' 46 Defense sacked Raider quarterbacks nine times with defensive end Richard Dent recording 4.5 sacks (half a season's worth for most guys) all by himself. They intercepted the Raiders three times, caused four fumbles, and held All-Pro running back Marcus Allen to 42 yards rushing en route to a convincing 17–6 victory. One could argue that the Raider mystique was never the same after that game.

The Bears lived up to their pre-season expectations and won the division with a 10–6 record, thereby earning a trip to RFK Stadium to play the two-time defending conference champion Washington Redskins. While the Redskins were hoping to go to their third Super Bowl in a row, the upstart Bears were looking to win their first playoff game in a generation. If any doubts lingered about the legitimacy of the Bears, none remained with their performance that afternoon. Continuing with the theme of playing with a chip on their shoulder against a favored and better known opponent, the Bears beat the Redskins in every facet of the game in a 24–19 victory on the road in a very hostile environment. They were younger and hungrier and provided a blueprint for success during the Ditka years—a strong ball control running game as Payton carried twenty-four times for 104 yards and a defense that completely stopped the run by holding future

Hall of Famer John Riggins to fifty yards on twenty-one carries. For his part, Redskin quarterback Joe Theisman would later say, "You'd like to think the corner[back]s were the ones you could exploit. But the only problem is that was hard to do when you're lying on your back."

The hard-fought victory earned the Bears a berth in the NFC championship game against San Francisco, again on the road, with the winner going on to the Super Bowl. The 49ers were the best team in the NFL that year, going 15–1. And although the Bears defense held tough in the first half, the Bears offense was unable to do anything against the 49ers' defense, and ultimately the best team won that day. San Francisco was going to the Super Bowl after a dominating 23–0 win. That game, however, and the humiliation of that loss would provide the final chip that the '84 Bears needed to work, improve, and take the necessary steps in the off season to prepare for a better outcome the next season.

CHAPTER 6

A Team for the Ages

As the Bears opened up training camp in July of 1985, an aura set in around the team and a buzz slowly began to creep across Chicagoland. Ditka and the Bears exuded confidence as it became clear that they channeled the pain and lessons learned from the loss in the NFC Championship to take the next step in both their physical and mental approach to the sport. The magazine stands were full of publications with the Bears on the cover, predicting Super Bowl glory. As a fan, I wasn't so sure—I had witnessed far too many sporting heartbreaks to think that a Chicago team could go all the way, and, besides, the 49ers still presented a huge obstacle. Either way, no one predicted the level of dominance the Bears would have in 1985.

The first sign of how special this team would become was a Week 3 nationally televised Thursday night game in Minnesota. For some reason, the Bears throughout the years always struggled in the Metrodome and this night was no exception. As an injured Jim McMahon sat there and watched, the Bears fell behind 17–9 in the third quarter. Having watched the offense unable to score a touchdown, McMahon pleaded with then begged Ditka to put him in the game. And when Ditka finally relented, the entire complexion of the game and season changed. On the very first play with McMahon in the game, he dropped back to pass as the Vikings sent an all out blitz with the linebacker charging hard, unblocked up the middle. In what would become a signature play of Walter Payton's career, and indication of what a great all-around player he was, Payton lowered his shoulder into the linebacker and cleanly blocked him, giving a stumbling McMahon enough time to look down the field and hit Willie Gault with a seventy-yard touchdown pass. Electrifying the entire team, the defense came through with an interception on the Vikings' next possession. McMahon immediately threw a touchdown on the next play and then the next possession as a 17–9 deficit quickly turned into a 30–17 lead within minutes. The Bears ultimately won 33–24 and a mystique was born. With a defense capable of shutting down the other team anytime they wanted, the Bears, maybe for the first time in their history, also possessed a well-rounded offense with a quick strike ability from anywhere on the field.

The quick strike, come-from-behind theme played itself out again the following week as the Redskins came to town looking for revenge. Facing a 10–0 deficit early in the second quarter, Willie Gault returned a kickoff ninety-nine yards for a touchdown, giving his team the spark they needed. By halftime, the score was 31–10 with an eventual final of 45–10. The Bears were 4–0 and only got better. In week six, the time came to return to San Francisco, where their Super Bowl dreams came to an end the year before in a 23–0 shutout. This, however, was a different Bear team. They were better, hungrier, and had Jim

McMahon back as starting quarterback. Having been shut out in the NFC Championship on the same field, the Bears went right down the field on their first possession with Walter Payton scoring a three-yard touchdown to cap the drive. The Bears' defense absolutely locked down the "West Coast" offense that day, sacking Joe Montana a then career-high seven times. The 49ers' only touchdown came on a defensive interception return, and with a 19–10 lead, the Bears' ball control offense went into gear, churning out an eight-minute drive in the fourth quarter culminating in a seventeen-yard run by Walter Payton, a run in which he dragged Ronnie Lott (widely considered the best safety in NFL history) into the end zone. There would be no stopping Payton or the Bears.

Before the age of the Internet and the explosion of cable and satellite TV, no highlight package shows were on the cable networks in 1985 like ESPN's NFL Primetime which became popular in the 1990s. So to watch the weekly highlights of the other games and get in-depth analysis of each game, you had to wait until Thursday Night when "Inside the NFL" came on HBO. And every Thursday, the more the season wore on, the more the show centered on the Bears. The best way before the information age to gauge a team's or athlete's popularity was simply by going to your mailbox every Thursday to get your *Sports Illustrated* magazine. After the 49er win, the Bears appeared on the cover and did so again a total of five times over the next fifteen weeks. With a picture of Jim McMahon and the title "Bears on the Prowl," they next captured the nation's attention on Monday Night Football. Chicago, already abuzz, now sensed we had a real shot at winning the Super Bowl. When Ditka put William "The Refrigerator" Perry at running back on the goal line that night and McMahon handed off the ball to him for a thundering touchdown, the rest of the nation would start buzzing for the Bears. They became the most popular team in North American sports.

The Bears started racking up wins at historic levels. At 9–0, they went on a three-game stretch in which they outscored their opponents by a combined 104–3, all with back-up quarterback Steve Fuller starting for the oft-injured McMahon. Sandwiched in the middle of that stretch was a trip to Texas Stadium to play the Dallas Cowboys. Although fading, a mystique still surrounded the Cowboys as well as Texas Stadium. The Cowboys were still "America's Team," and fans proclaimed the hole in the roof of Texas Stadium existed so God could watch His favorite football team. With the backdrop of this aura and McMahon out, odds makers made the Cowboys slight favorites, which just enlarged the chip on Ditka's, Buddy Ryan's, and the rest of the Bears' shoulders.

I remember expecting the Bears to win because, by this point, you didn't think they could lose. But no one expected what actually ended up happening. In what would be Dallas' worst home loss ever, the Bears simply crushed the Cowboys 44–0—setting the tone by scoring the first two touchdowns of the game on defense and knocking out Cowboy quarterback Danny White with a concussion. It was almost surreal in the fourth quarter as the Bears fans took over Texas Stadium after the Cowboys fans departed for home early. Dallas was no longer America's Team. When I started following football at six years old up until that day, the Cowboys were always a team that you feared—but no longer. Much like the

Raiders two years earlier, the Cowboys' mystique of that era was never the same once the Bears finished them off.

The talk around town and the football world now was whether or not the Bears could become only the second team in NFL history to go undefeated. With a 12–0 record, the Bears played again on Monday Night Football, this time on the road against the Miami Dolphins whose 1972 squad coincidentally was that team which had gone undefeated. Suffice it to say, this wasn't the Bears' night as Dolphin quarterback Dan Marino would have what would become the defining game of his Hall of Fame career. The Dolphins would shred the Bears' vaunted 46 Defense, scoring 31 points by halftime—more than they allowed in the last six games combined! The only drama really left was whether or not Walter Payton, then in his eleventh season and ancient by running back standards, would break the NFL record for most 100-yard rushing games in a row. He did just that, rushing for 121 yards and in the process crossing 100 yards for the eleventh time consecutively.

The ironic thing about the loss was that the typical "doom and gloom" mentality that sets in upon Chicago after a big loss never materialized. Even though we had suffered without a champion for twenty-two years, even though we had experienced so many heartbreaks in the early '80s with DePaul, the Sox, and then the Cubs, the Bears to us were above it all. If anything, the thinking went that this loss would be good for them. It would help them to refocus and get them angry in the process; they'd learn and improve from their mistakes. For their part, the Bears' players were so concerned about the loss that after getting back to Chicago in the early hours of Tuesday after the Monday Night game, they promptly went out that morning to record "The Super Bowl Shuffle." Think about that for a minute: here was a team coming off a loss, still with three regular games left and then the playoffs, going out and recording a music video about the Super Bowl—a game the Bears organization had never played in the nineteen-year history of the event.

With the "Super Bowl Shuffle" playing in tape decks and VCRs and on radios and televisions (MTV) nationwide, the Bears saturated the sporting nation's conscience and really the nation as a whole. But obviously the euphoria existed nowhere near that of Chicago's—where you couldn't read a newspaper, watch the news, go to school, work, the store, or anywhere for that matter where the Bears weren't topic number one. They won their last three regular season games, went into the playoffs 15–1, and were ready to take their game to an even higher level. Any anxiety that existed about another Chicago postseason flop went away when the Bears opened up the playoffs with a dominating 21–0 win against the Giants and again the following week when they humiliated the Rams 24–0 to win the NFC Championship. The defense became the only unit in NFL history to record back-to-back shutouts in the playoffs, and, really, the only question for us as fans in the run-up to the Super Bowl was how badly they'd beat the AFC Champion New England Patriots.

As Bears fans, most of us were disappointed that the Patriots had upset the Dolphins in the AFC Championship because we wanted another shot at the Dolphins to avenge the Bears' only loss. Regardless, it didn't matter who they played, as I'm convinced not a team in NFL history would have beaten the

Bears on that day. And even when an early Walter Payton fumble led to a 3–0 deficit, we were just waiting for the inevitable onslaught by the Bears. The score was 13–3 at the end of the first quarter and 23–3 by halftime. Patriot starting quarterback Tony Eason is probably still having nightmares, as it seemed like every time he dropped back to pass, five Bears used him as a tackling dummy in the backfield. At the half, the Patriots had -19 total yards and only one first down.

With the defense completely in lockdown mode, the Bears offense took advantage of a Patriot defense over-keyed on stopping Walter Payton to exploit them in every other area. McMahon, in particular, played well with 256 passing yards and two rushing touchdowns. As a fan, my only disappointment was that Walter Payton never did score a touchdown. In three goal-line situations, the Bears used Payton as a decoy. The best opportunity came on first and goal toward the end of the third quarter when Ditka, who was caught up in the Fridge-hype like everybody else, had McMahon give the ball to William Perry for a one-yard touchdown run. To this day, when I watch a replay of the game on the NFL Network, some small part of me still hopes this time it might be different, that it might be Payton scoring the touchdown.

But nonetheless, we as Chicagoans finally had our Super Bowl champion. For anybody under the age of thirty in 1985, this was our first memory of one of our teams ending the season as the best in the world; what an incredible feeling as a fan, for so many reasons: the way they won, the personalities they had, how they embodied everything Chicago prides itself on. Because it had been so long in between titles, because the Bears organization hasn't won a Super Bowl since, and because Chicago is a Bears town—that team twenty-five years later is still legendary with those of us who remember that special time in our lives. We learned the value of setting goals and the reward that came with following through with the necessary effort, determination, and sacrifice to achieve those goals.

CHAPTER 7

The Aftermath

The 1985 Chicago Bears were not only dominant; they were the youngest team in the National Football League. This was a team built to win multiple Super Bowls over the next decade. With a strong 6–0 start to the '86 season, including a stretch in weeks 4–6 where they outscored their opponents 87–13, it looked like another Super Bowl trophy would be won. Unfortunately, and unbelievably, they never got back to the Super Bowl and really would never come close. While the 1985 Bears were a textbook example of charting a path to and then achieving success, the post–Super Bowl Bears provided a case study and life lesson of how success can ruin a person. Ego, selfishness, a need for the spotlight, and an overall loss of focus in staying true to what led them to the top all helped to undermine and keep the Bears from ever coming close to duplicating their success again. If the '85 Bears were a rock band, they would have made a great "Behind the Music" feature for VH1, a documentary inevitably depicting a group's rise to the top followed by a fall resulting from inner-dissension, over-indulgence, and a clashing of egos.

In Week 7, they were stunned in Minnesota 23–7 (the same Viking team they beat two weeks before 23–0) and lost 20–17 at home on Monday night two weeks later to the Rams (the same Ram team they dominated 24–0 the year before in the NFC Championship game). Three weeks later, the Bears lost Jim McMahon for the rest of the season with a separated throwing shoulder on a wicked cheap shot by Packer Charles Martin. If you use NFL history as your guide, the one constant with teams that win multiple Super Bowls in short periods of time (i.e. dynasties such as the '60s Packers, '70s Steelers, '80s 49ers, '90s Cowboys, or '00s Patriots) is that every one of those teams enjoyed consistency and health at the quarterback position. On top of a mounting list of other injuries, McMahon would never be the same player again. Teammates, namely defensive tackle Dan Hampton, began to lose faith in McMahon, questioning his work ethic to recover from injuries and his training regimen to prevent them. The winning aura surrounding McMahon began to fade and, along with him, the would-be Bears dynasty.

Although the defense was still stout and allowed an NFL record low in points in 1986, they also lacked the bite and attacking mentality they had in '85. Buddy Ryan, the architect of the famed 46 Defense, left after the Super Bowl to become head coach of the Eagles and was replaced by defensive coordinator Vince Tobin, a capable albeit less aggressive persona than Ryan. While they finished the regular season 14–2 and won their third division title in a row, they by no means had the same swagger going into the playoffs in '86. Sure enough, without a McMahon-led offense or Ryan-led defense, they were dealt a devastating 27–13 loss to the Redskins.

The opening week of Monday Night Football to kick off the 1987 season featured the winners of the two previous Super

Bowls: the Bears and the New York Giants. For one game at least, it looked like the '85 Bears were back as they terrorized the Giants in winning 34–19. The next week they beat the Buccaneers 20–3 and reestablished themselves with two thorough victories. Then the NFL Players Union went on strike and, as a result, the League brought in replacement players. In a move that Mike Singletary said was the biggest mistake of Ditka's coaching career, Ditka sided with management and embraced the "Spare Bears," calling them "his players." A fractured relationship between Da Coach and the real Bears resulted upon their return in Week 6. The team that started off the season so ferocious now stumbled into wins against sub par teams—wins closer than they should have been. And when they lost 41–0 at San Francisco on Monday night in Week 13, it became painfully obvious that the 1987 season would end in much the same way the '86 season ended, and sure enough it did—with another home playoff loss to the Redskins in what would be Walter Payton's last game as he retired after a no-regrets thirteen-year career in which he gave the very best of himself in every game he ever played.

A third home playoff loss in a row in 1988, this time to the San Francisco 49ers in the NFC Championship, marked the official end of the dynasty that never was, as well as the end of McMahon era in Chicago. The outspoken McMahon simply wore out his welcome in Chicago by this point. Always brash and cocky, he never hesitated to loudly question ownership, management, and coaching. After 1985, his mounting injuries and poor preparation caught up to him. With two bad, season-ending playoff performances in 1987 and '88 dogging him, the

Bears traded McMahon before the 1989 season to San Diego. The Bears would return to the playoffs two more times under Ditka in 1990 and '91, but those teams were an older and far less talented version, neither squad being a true contender. After a 5–11 1992 record in which they lost eight of their last nine, Mike Ditka, the longest tenured and winningest coach in franchise history other than his mentor George Halas, was fired. With fans gathered and chanting his name outside Halas Hall, a very emotional and tearful Ditka gave the following sendoff in a press conference that had grown men crying all over Chicago:

"... Of course I have to thank Coach Halas. I guess you've got to thank the players most because they make it happen. I was blessed. I came here and I inherited a hell of a football team. Man, you've got Walter Payton, you've got a hell of a football team. We drafted some good kids, we took a run. Pretty good ... we did a pretty good job. Players make it happen. Had some great assistant coaches and respect every one of them. I really loved every one I've ever had. Disagreements or no disagreements, they've been very vital in my life. I've had my run-ins with you guys [referring to the media] and I've had a lot of support from you. I appreciate it and I thank you. I thank the fans of this city. You know, the Bears will come back. Mike Ditka will survive. I will land on my feet. There's no problem about that. I don't worry about that. I worry about how this organization is perceived. I believe it will go forward and try to do the things necessary to make the adjustments to get through the '90s the way it should. I would hope that. It's pretty hard to erase 17 years. Not much else I can say but thank you, I appreciate it and this, too, shall pass."

And with that, the "Chicago Tough" era for the Bears in my lifetime concluded and almost twenty years later I'm still waiting for it to return. The Ditka and Payton years were an era initially showing the rewards from living up to one's potential. Conversely, I saw how promise and potential can unravel with a loss of focus as well as getting away from your roots. Prior to '85, the focus was primarily on the goal of winning. After '85, the focus shifted to priorities and personality conflicts outside of winning. While the departure of Ryan and, more importantly, the injuries of McMahon significantly impacted the Bears' inability to get back to and win another Super Bowl, other issues played a role as well. Overindulgence and excess in the media and commercial endorsements came to define the late '80s Bears, including Ditka, who seemed to be in every commercial and endorse every product from cars to antihistamines. About the only item Ditka didn't endorse was female pantyhose, as Joe Namath famously did in the 1970s. By the late '80s, I almost had to turn off my television during commercial breaks because of the sick feeling I'd get due to the over-saturation of Ditka.

Lack of preparation from McMahon in reporting to training camp in 1986 out of shape and overweight didn't help his injury issues. Infighting between players as well as players and management, plus a lack of commitment from management to keep and reward key players from the '85 team (Wilbur Marshall and Willie Gault were allowed to leave via free agency after '87), all contributed to the implosion of the Bears after 1985. Those are all cautionary tales about how not to handle success once you achieve it—in every area of life.

The aftermath of the implosion of the Super Bowl XX champion Bears also demonstrates that positive outcomes can become an outgrowth of enduring and persevering through adversity.   Cornerback Leslie Frazier blew out his knee in the Super Bowl and would never play another game. Frazier, always active in the Fellowship for Christian Athletes throughout his career, is now considered one of the best defensive coordinators in NFL with the Minnesota Vikings.   In 1988, he began his coaching career by becoming the first head coach at Trinity College, a Christian institution in Illinois, where Frazier built the program from the ground up and won a pair of Northern Illinois Intercollegiate Conference titles.   Defensive lineman Tyrone Keys was disappointed after he was traded from the Bears to the last place Tampa Bay Buccaneers after the '85 season. But Keys made his home in Tampa when he retired after the 1988 season and founded All Sports Community Service. All Sports, is a non-profit organization, aimed at providing students, financially and emotionally, with opportunities at higher education. The program instills values in the students by ensuring they contribute to their communities through volunteerism, community service and mentoring. In the arc of fate, Frazier signed many of Keys' students to play at Trinity. And finally, for his part, Ditka has used his post-coaching career to give back by founding Gridiron Greats. Gridiron Greats provides financial assistance and coordinates social services to retired, and often disabled, former NFL players of yesteryear. These older players, while contributing to the NFL's status as the most popular sport in America, didn't make anywhere near the money, nor have the benefits, that players today enjoy.

CHAPTER 8

Champaign Times

I enrolled in the University of Illinois in the fall of 1992. Looking back, I loved everything about U of I and enjoyed every bit of my college experience, from the social scene to the academic setting to the athletic arena. I blossomed and truly became comfortable as a "person with a disability" in college. The social scene at Illinois was one I embraced in every aspect. Although I had dated sporadically after my injury, I had my first serious dating relationships at Illinois, the first, a two-year relationship that spanned my junior and senior years. I developed some of the closest friendships I've ever had in my life at U of I. With regards to academics, I embraced the art of "time management" in prioritizing how to excel in the classes I took without becoming over-burdened, eventually graduating with honors with a Bachelor's Degree in Sociology (1994) and then a Master's Degree in Journalism (1995).

But the rugby court is where I would surpass heights and accomplish accolades I never thought nor dreamed of when I began playing at Illinois in October of 1992. I played team sports growing up, mostly baseball, and always enjoyed the camaraderie, bonding, and friendships. Playing for Illinois was no exception. But at Illinois, I realized for the first time the importance of surrounding yourself with talented, hardworking, and ethical peers to become successful in your life endeavors. If you want to be mediocre and settle for less than your potential, then surround yourself with mediocre people. If you want to be a loser by not fulfilling your potential, then surround yourself with losers. At U of I, I surrounded myself for the first time in my life with nothing but winners in my peer group.

I developed friendships and relationships lasting to this day and I learned from my teammates the values of selflessness in working together to accomplish common goals. The core group of players (Shawn Meredith, Paul LeVasseur, Norm Lyduch, and I) would play together for the next three years, and I became best friends with two teammates I lived with, Pat Faherty and Dave Ford. I learned a lot from all these guys. Aside from excelling in rugby, Meredith, LeVasseur, and Lyduch were all dual athletes who competed in track. Meredith won a combined 5 gold medals at the '92 Barcelona and '96 Atlanta Paralympic Games. LeVasseur also found the time to earn his MBA at Illinois. I learned more about hard work from these guys than any other peers I had up to this point of my life.

Pat Faherty, a fellow 1.5, had more rugby experience and was four years older than me, so I studied his game both on the court and off. Off the court, his humility and good nature stood out most to me. Although he won just about every 1.5 All-Tournament award back then, he stayed humble and never let the accolades go to his head. On the court, he destroyed me during my first couple of years. The enduring memory from my rookie year in Chicago was matching up against Pat and his pink rugby chair when we played Illinois and how that pink chair spent a lot of time bashing, knocking, and blocking my chair. When I saw him outside my room at U of I for the first time and realized he was living two doors down from me, I quipped that we'd be able to get along only if he kept his pink chair away from me. In the years since, I've seen more resilience in Pat than anybody else I've ever met. Diagnosed with a rare heart ailment in 1998, he's been in and out of the hospital numerous times for open-heart procedures, and yet the guy continues to battle onward with the support of his wife Traci and young daughter Lilly.

Dave Ford is simply the most determined guy I've ever met and he taught me what being driven is all about. We were suite mates and I saw that guy study day and night to not only earn an accounting degree from U of I, which is no small feat, but also pass all four parts of his CPA exam on the first attempt—a feat only seventeen percent of those taking the exam accomplish. He would literally take twenty minutes to push up a hill while passing up an offer to get up the hill in five minutes by having someone push him. Years later, his wife told me a story of him falling out of bed and then having leg spasms, preventing him from transferring back into bed. Instead of allowing his physical therapist wife to assist him back into the bed, he slept on the floor until the next morning when his spasms subsided and he was able to lift himself.

With teammates like these guys and a new found teachable spirit on my part, experiencing future success proved inevitable. A goal we all had in our first team meeting in October of 1992 was qualifying for the National Championships held the following

April in Tampa, Florida. This goal would be no small feat as only the top two out of our eight-team region qualified. Further complicating the goal, the two top-ranked teams from our region, Minnesota and North Dakota, were national powers, having finished the '92 season in third and fifth respectively. Both teams dominated our region in qualifying for Nationals five straight years since the first National Championships in 1988. And at the '92 regional championships the previous April, neither Illinois nor my Chicago team came within fifteen goals of either Minnesota or North Dakota. We were a bunch of young college kids without much experience hoping to become the first university to qualify for nationals. To do so, we needed to beat at least one of two much older and more experienced teams. I remember looking around the room at the meeting and thinking we had a lot of talent. But as we talked about getting to Tampa as our goal, I remember thinking that I had no idea how we could get past either one of those teams.

For me as an individual player, I was definitely up and coming going into my second year. I won the "Most Improved Player" Award as a rookie in Chicago and went from being thirteenth on the depth roster on a fourteen-man team in Chicago to a player in the main rotation going into my first year as a member of the Illini. If you would've asked me at the time, I would've told you that I was a serious competitor—intent on getting better. But in retrospect, my work ethic lacked the necessary effort to become a consistent contributor. With one year of experience, my "chair skills" and speed improved. Additionally, I had more endurance and practiced harder. But I certainly was not committed "off the court." I seldom worked out even though we had access to a tremendous and accessible training facility. And frequently I'd just go through the motions during our Saturday morning practices after a few hours of sleep and a hard night of partying down on Green Street in Champaign.

Our team had a decent, if not stellar, regular season, but we started coming together on and off the court as the regular season wound down. Road trips always seemed to be an adventure with this bunch. The heart of the season is January through March, always providing interesting weather in the Midwest. We usually loaded up a couple of Chevy Suburbans with a trailer and made the two-hour drive to O'Hare Airport outside of Chicago to fly to whatever destination (Atlanta, Tampa, Minneapolis, Toronto, Houston, Denver, etc.) for an upcoming tournament. And often times we ended up stranded in an airport somewhere because of snow, and when that happened some version of a rugby game or wheelchair dodge ball might break out in the terminal. On occasion, we flew a puddle-jumper out of the tiny Willard Airport in Champaign to O'Hare for our connection. And it was on the puddle jumpers where some of my most enduring memories of traveling took place.

After a 1993 tournament where we made a long drive from Champaign to Atlanta, fellow 1.5 Pat Faherty and I spent an extra day to hang out around town and relax. We flew back with Pat booking the tickets and because we were broke college students, we took the cheap route, Atlanta to Nashville to Champaign. I remember looking at the fifty-seat prop plane out of the terminal window and remarking how it would be the smallest plane

I ever flew in. My angst grew when Pat proceeded to tell me that the plane was a "DC 10" compared to our connecting plane in Nashville. *Great,* I thought, and of course the weather was atrocious although, somehow, they allowed the plane to take off. We weren't in the air ten minutes when severe turbulence hit us. Thirty minutes in, the only flight attendant on the small flight asked those of us in the front of the plane if we were going to need our barf bags because they were running out of them in the back of the plane. The lady next to me sobbed like a child, and across the aisle the lady next to Pat bowed in fervent prayer. Surely the plane was going to fall apart in mid-air! This was the only time over the course of dozens, if not hundreds, of flights in my career where I truly felt I was going to die. Somehow we landed safely in Nashville but now the time came to get on an even smaller plane—a twenty-seater without even a flight attendant! I tried talking Pat into renting a car and driving the six hours home. But he coaxed me onto the plane where they had to put our wheelchairs in the lavatory because the baggage area underneath was so small. Not yet a Christian, I still managed to thank God once we finally arrived safely in Champaign.

Another traveling adventure happened en route to the 1994 Regionals. We took an American Eagle puddle jumper from Willard to O'Hare to connect to our American flight headed for the Minneapolis tournament. Sure enough, the wind and snow picked up that morning and whiteout conditions blanketed the state with airports, including O'Hare, shut down. Our dilemma facing us when O'Hare was shut down was that we were 15,000 feet in the air above it! So we circled and circled and circled while waiting for a window that never opened. By this time, and with fuel running low, we were forced into an emergency landing at the closest airport in Bloomington, Illinois (only a fifty minute drive from Champaign).

Upon landing, airport personnel now had to get us in from the runway in whiteout conditions. The small prop planes and airports don't have jetways connecting the plane to the terminal. Usually we, as quads, transferred from our wheelchair to an aisle chair where two men (one front and back) carried the aisle chair up at least eight stairs into the plane. They reversed the process when we arrived at our destination. But now, we were to be carried out of the plane and down the stairs in a blizzard. They wrapped blankets around us so tightly anybody watching had to think some sort of hostage crisis unfolded in front of them. Two of our guys ended up being accidentally dumped into the snow. Once in the Bloomington Airport, which is slightly bigger than a doctor's office, I declared I would never again fly in a propeller-powered plane. Six hours later, they finally opened up the airport and we continued on our journey. The funny thing is how analogous those journeys were to those we go through in life. Things don't go as planned, and the path usually gets chaotic. But by enduring it, you'll usually get to your goal or final destination. In this case, these types of trips provided great bonding opportunities with my teammates.

A month before the '93 regional championships, our sole focus in practice became beating North Dakota, the most likely path for us to get to nationals. North Dakota had one real dominant player (a 3.5) and ran a 3.5, 3, 1, .5 lineup (remember, each player is given a point classification based on the level of disability with 3.5 being the most functional and .5 being the least with no more than 8 points and four players from each team on the court). So the key was stopping the 3.5 who grew accustomed to running all over us. Our coach devised a scheme: triple-teaming their 3.5 by tying him up prior to the inbound pass from their 3, while our fourth player roamed between North Dakota's two remaining players on the court. The risk, of course, in triple teaming one opposing player was leaving only one of our players to cover the remaining two opponents on the court.

Additionally, we could not make chair contact until the ref handed the in-bounder the ball and blew the whistle to start the play. Our three guys needed quickness and incredible maneuverability in staying close enough to lock the 3.5 down once the ref blew the whistle. In theory, we'd lock him down with three players and then leave our two least functioning players on him, thereby releasing our fastest guy to try to cover the field two on three once the play began.

We ran three main lines that year—2.5, 2.5, 2, 1 and 2.5, 2.5, 1.5, 1.5 (me), as well as 3.0, 2.5, 2, 1. Still a part-time player that year, I relished my role and the playing time I received after sitting the bench most of my rookie season. Our balanced lineups and speed, at least on paper, seemed like it would work well against their unbalanced line. We spent a solid month every Tuesday night, Thursday night, and Saturday morning working this press. Once again, the learned art of repetition, doing something over

over again, lead to perfection and proved an invaluable tool on the playing court as well as in life. We brought stronger functioning paraplegics from the basketball team to simulate North Dakota's 3.5. Our thought process was if we could stop a para with too much function to be eligible for quad rugby, then certainly we'd stop a quad, regardless of his function level.

On the Friday night of Regionals which U of I hosted in front of a raucous home crowd, all of our heart and hard work was to be put to the test. We played the heavily favored Wallbangers from North Dakota with a trip to Tampa on the line. They say the definition of luck is when preparation meets opportunity. Well our team definitely came out prepared and, with North Dakota overlooking us, the opportunity for a big upset presented itself. Again, this was the first time anybody in the country saw this defensive press and, thus, North Dakota had no idea what hit them or how to handle it. We took the ball out of their best player's hands and forced his teammates to beat us. With deafening crowd noise, North Dakota panicked, and when they adjusted to our defense, they trailed 29–20. But just when we thought our time had come, they started chipping into our lead, whittling it down to 4, then 3, then 2, and then 1. Despite a furious Wallbanger rush at the end, we held on to win 36–35 as the crowd went crazy and we rushed center court.

Although we fell short at Nationals, we were the first collegiate team to compete at that level—a distinction not matched until the University of Arizona qualified in 2005. Most of the guys, including me, were just happy to be there. Of a twelve-man roster, only one of our guys had ever competed at Nationals—

Pat Faherty with his club team from Boston in 1991. We played a little awestruck as a result of our inexperience. None of us to that point ever witnessed so many talented teams and players assembled together in one place. Plus, taking a bunch of college kids from Illinois to Tampa in April after a harsh winter—well, it was kind of difficult for spring break not to break out.

Nationals were not without on-court drama for me as I harkened back to the feeling from being cut from my high school baseball team. Our second line that season was my line. Faherty, our other 1.5, however, relayed to me before Nationals that our coach didn't feel comfortable going to that lineup in a close game because he lacked confidence in me. Well, that came as a blow to me. I gained confidence with my playing time steadily improving throughout the season. But my confidence gave way to self-doubt and hurt upon hearing this news. We found ourselves in a one-goal game late in the fourth quarter during our last game at Nationals. My line was in the game when my coach decided to sub me out of the game with our less-functioning Class 1. I felt completely humiliated—my team now short-pointed (less than 8 points on the court) with 7.5 points on the court because the coach lacked confidence in me. Not the first time this happened, Shawn Meredith and I would often joke that I became conditioned like one of Pavlov's dogs. No matter where on the court, and whether we were playing or not, I would automatically head to the closest bench if I heard the buzzer. But getting pulled at such a key moment on a big stage like Nationals was no laughing matter. Twenty-one at the time and still somewhat immature, I felt disrespected and a little more entitled than I should have, declaring after Nationals that my rugby career was finished, just like when I walked away from baseball in high school, never again to play the sport of my youth and first love of my life.

Again at a sporting crossroads, I drew from the maturity that comes from experience as well as lessons learned from my past, my upbringing, and those teams I followed growing up. Not only would I not quit the game, but I became determined to use the perceived slight of my coach to develop a "chip on the shoulder" mentality in committing myself to excellence in the sport. I wasn't bitter but rather motivated to push myself to achieve success. Never again would I be subbed out for a player with less function. A value instilled in me by my parents that was re-enforced during this time frame and later reaffirmed through my understanding as a Christian of biblical principles was one of accountability and taking responsibility for your own career and future. Looking back, our Class 1 outworked me in practice and in his off-court training. He deserved that playing time more than I did! My parents never accepted excuses or blaming others for my problems. A constant theme throughout the Bible is that of inward renewal, growth, and responsibility as opposed to pointing fingers and blaming others. I learned from my parents, and then sports, not to put yourself in positions or situations where others can dictate your outcome. Since that time, I've never blamed a coach or a ref for my circumstances. Many times as a fan or directly as a player, I've witnessed a referee make a bad call or calls that influence the outcome of a game or series. But regardless of any media outcry or whining from players, it all comes down to personal accountability—your role, not the coach or ref, in influencing your outcome. Sure, the ref may have made a mistake, but as a player you probably made ten mistakes prior to the bad call. Had you not made those mistakes, the game wouldn't have been in a position to be decided by a referee's whistle or a coach's or teammate's mistake.

The off season and summer of 1993 was spent mostly enjoying life on a college campus with a lighter summer crowd and without the pressure of taking a full course load. Some of the best times of my life were the three summers spent in Champaign, Illinois. I also committed, for the first time, to a training regimen consisting of weight training for strength and endurance. Many of my other teammates staying on campus for the summer months would participate as well, and we also had weekly informal practices and scrimmages.

Going into my third season, I was finally a starter and played every minute of every game although mostly as the result of a number of last season's players graduating. Nonetheless, my confidence in my game began to grow. We beat North Dakota once more at '94 Regionals as they failed yet again to figure out our press. But we missed our opportunity to advance to Nationals for the second year in a row. With only six teams in our region that year, we played a round robin format over a three-day weekend with the two best records advancing to Nationals. North Dakota ended up beating perennial Regional Champion Minnesota by one while Minnesota beat us quite handily, with us losing the three-way tie breaker based on overall point differential between the three teams.

Our final game at '94 Regionals provided me with another confidence booster as I continued the climb as a solid player. We faced Chicago, a friendly rival of ours. In a close game, their plan revolved around forcing me to handle the ball as they thought I was the weak link (as my coach did at Nationals the year before). They figured if they could take away our two most functioning and best players, they could force the ball into my hands and create turnovers by putting pressure on me similar to our North Dakota game plan. Continually I heard their coach admonishing his team to "Let Renje handle the ball!" And continually I proved up to the task of either beating their defensive pressure for a score or finding an open teammate to pass the ball off to for a goal. With the game in hand and a little over a minute to go, I wheeled past their bench and yelled "Let Renje handle the ball!," which generated a bit of a chuckle from their coach. Yet another building block was laid in my confidence which would shape me for years to come.

Off the court, I consistently gained confidence as well. My social life was as good as ever. Although I always had a pretty large circle of friends in high school, most of those relationships were pretty superficial, as I found out once the majority of those "friends" abandoned me after my injury. By the spring of 1994, I had a well-rounded group of friends including my teammates. Graduating with a B.A., I was accepted by the journalism department into a very competitive and intense twelve-month graduate program. Illinois's master's program in journalism was ranked number five in the country and they accepted only twenty or so students (we had eighteen) each year out of several hundred applicants. My greatest accomplishment, at the time, also provided an even greater challenge.

While I was tested with the rigors of a tough twelve-month academic stretch in front of me, our rugby team looked head on at our toughest challenge as well. Our '94–'95 team on paper would be the most talented team ever fielded by U of I wheelchair rugby. The core of our team had now been together for three years—we were all better as we routinely trained together in the off season and more experienced as well. Further, three new players arrived, one of which was a three-year starter from Chicago, and all had function, ability, and speed. Realignment of the regions, however, placed the defending National Champion Tennessee Quad Crushers in our region. Additionally, the two best players from our old nemesis at North Dakota left to play for Minnesota, who was already the five-time defending regional champion. So much like the preseason meeting two years before, I wondered how we would crack that top two and qualify for Nationals despite the talent, depth, and experience that we had in the room.

Looking back, that squad was the most talented of our U of I teams and also the closest in terms of chemistry and on-court continuity. We were all young, having common ground with being students while living within a ten-minute walk of each other. So we played together, studied together, and partied together. Chemistry is important in team sports and translates into other areas of life like family and business. If you want to be successful, you not only need to have talented people around you, you also need to develop deep relationships with those people. Once doing so, the task becomes easier to put your selfish desires aside for greater, common goals. Our team realized our collective capabilities as we set out for Corpus

Christi, Texas, for a tournament in early February, one month before Regionals.

Two years before, our Illini team left the frozen tundra of the Midwest for Nationals in Tampa and we treated the trip like spring break. This time around, we treated it more as a business trip; the tourney would be a Nationals-type tournament with high caliber teams competing. As the seventh seed in the eight-team field, our first game on Friday night would be against the number two seeded Quadzilla out of Northern California. They were an aging team but nonetheless loaded, as they would end that season ranked number three after winning the 1990 National Championship and finishing National runner-up in '91, '92, and '93. I remember thinking before the game that a victory would be staying within ten goals of them. Clearly, they overlooked us and expected at some point to put together a run, but it would be a run that would never come. We went toe to toe with them, matched them goal for goal, and ended the thirty-two-minute regulation tied and headed for a three-minute overtime—then a second, third, fourth, fifth, and finally sixth overtime. We stayed with them the entire game, and with every other team watching, we held them off in the furious last ten seconds of the sixth overtime and won 54–53. At the time, it was the longest and highest scoring game of all time. Our starting lineup went the whole way and we were gassed. Afterward, I asked Meredith, our 2.5, "Do you *realize* who we just *beat*?!" and we just embraced.

Now a budding, if unknown, star in my fourth season, I had yet to be named to an All-Tournament team. That streak was not to be broken when they announced the All-Tourney team after the title game. However, quite the confidence boost came my way as I sat near the top-ranked Tampa Generals who were in the midst of winning their third National Title in four years. When they announced the team, their coach, also the National team coach and someone I never had a conversation with to that point, told me, "They just don't know who you are yet, Bill." Well, that was all I needed. *The head coach of the Tampa Generals knows who I am—awesome!* I thought. As a team, we stood ready for the colossal task of trying to finish in the top two in our region to qualify for Nationals.

Going into our Saturday afternoon regional semifinal against Minnesota, I experienced equal amounts of excitement and nervousness. I've since realized that in athletics, like business, a healthy and balanced combination of nervousness and fear is a good thing. The key is striking a balance. Too little fear and nervousness can lead to a "letting down of your guard," meaning a lack of focus and complacency. Too much fear and nervousness can lead to "stage fright" and a poor performance based on giving in to those emotions and "choking" in the big moment. This game would be the ultimate in our team's finding that balance, and the result provided the peak for our squad's three-year run.

My last Regional as a member of the Illini was upon me, and with it came my last shot at Nationals with the team I had grown with over the previous three seasons. Our team was amped up, as a win against Minnesota in the semifinals would put us in the regional championship. But a loss would end our season, as only the top two regional finishers went to Nationals in Denver. We were playing the six-time defending regional champion who had absorbed our previous rival, North Dakota's, two best players. Minnesota was a team whose two best players were among the most feared and intimidating that I had ever seen. Both looked like hockey goons and neither was afraid to intimidate with a healthy dose of trash talk. We were prepared for anything as the game started. We jumped on them early and then waited for them to respond, which never happened. They were older and slower; we were younger and faster, taking their heart out with every minute that ticked off the clock. The rout was on and unbelievably we used all of our skills against Minnesota in a 47–26 thrashing.

That night we celebrated going to Nationals for the second time in three years. We then went out on Sunday morning and were soundly whipped by the defending champion Tennessee Quad Crushers for the Regional Championship. Even though we stood little chance, I was humiliated by my performance, the result of a late night of partying prior to the title game. At that point, I committed to always being at my peak, mentally, emotionally, and physically. My performance in the title game notwithstanding, I did achieve a personal milestone by being named to the All-Tournament team—the first of what would be thirty-six in my career. Regardless, in the future, if I would lose or not have my best performance, a lack of preparation would not be the reason. I committed to taking my game, as well as anything I did in life, to the highest level possible. After Nationals, I returned to campus to get ready for finals and then to write my Master's thesis over the summer—my final requirement to receive my M.S. in journalism.

That summer, my last on a college campus, I relished every moment knowing that in August I'd be moving on to the next phase of my life. From an athletic standpoint, my rugby career really started to take off. I met and dated an All-American runner from Michigan State that summer. She lived in Champaign and I learned a lot from her on how to really train and take care of your body by watching what you eat, getting your proper rest, as well as getting your mind right mentally to compete at a high level. I graduated from my Master's program in August. With a bachelor's degree the year before, I became the first member of my family on either my dad's or mom's side to graduate from college. When I went across the stage in a cap and gown to receive my degree, I, for the first time, felt like I had redeemed myself to my parents for all the anguish I had put them through as a teenager. Everything I set out to do from the time of being shot was done, in my mind, to try to make amends and to make my parents proud of me. To see their joy made the occasion extra special for me. With the U of I chapter then closed in my life, I soon underwent the greatest transformation of my life.

SECTION IV

The Glory Years (1996–2000)

I n August of 1995, I returned home to Tinley Park after
graduation. Although unsure of my long-term plan, I took a
three-month internship at the CBS affiliate in Chicago in the sports
department under Tim Weigel. In an era before the dominance of
ESPN, your daily dose of sports news came at the end of the 6:00
and 10:00 news. Weigel had been the face of the Chicago sports
media since I became a fan in the late '70s. He popularized his
Thursday night "Wiegel Wieners" segment by spotlighting sports
gaffes and blunders from the previous week. He was as well-known
and popular around Chicagoland as a sports personality like Chris
Berman became nationally with ESPN. So I felt honored to learn
under him at a time when I considered a career behind the camera
in a sports department although my education was in the realm of
print journalism. I interned on the production side and learned the
mechanics of producing sports segments. Along the way, I enjoyed
the opportunity to attend Bears practices and games at field-level
while rubbing elbows with players. Beyond that internship, however,
I lacked a long-term vision, not fully convinced I wanted to pursue
journalism fulltime.

Although only gone for three years, it seemed like I had not
lived at home for thirty years. Though my past was there, I knew

my future awaited me elsewhere. Most of my friends before I went to college had long since moved on to the next stage of life and those friends from U of I either moved on as well or were still in Champaign. The girl I dated during the summer returned to Michigan State and I felt somewhat alone and on my own for the first time in my life. I remember going to a local sports bar that I hung out at with my friends before going away to school. Now, at the same bar, I mostly ran into my younger brother's peers while wondering what happened to all mine. The town I knew from the age of ten had also changed as well. Tinley once had charm with only a handful of restaurants. I remember a time where you couldn't go out to eat or to a grocery store without seeing someone you knew and chances were high when you stopped at a traffic light that you'd know the person in the car next to you. Growing up, Tinley was a mix of suburbia and wide-open fields, trails as well as wooded areas. Kids rode their bikes for miles in every direction uninhibited by traffic congestion. We enjoyed dirt hills and trails down the street from my house where we'd sled in the winter and ride dirt bikes in the summer. A retention pond aptly named Chevy Lake, due to its location behind the Chevrolet dealer, froze in the winter for hockey games and provided neighborhood kids a fishing hole in the summer. A Facebook page called "I hung out at Chevy Lake" exists today where more than sixty members look back in fondness at our memories there. But the story of my hometown mirrors those of many who grew up in the '60s, '70s, or '80s. A saturation of commercial development began during my high school years, making the town today almost unrecognizable to me.

So I began to do some soul searching during the fall of 1995. I thought about my life and all that I accomplished in the previous half-decade, all the goals I still maintained, and yet a part of me remained empty. Don't get me wrong, I was not on the verge of any kind of depression. My still strong support network included a backbone of family support and some solid albeit distant relationships coupled with my athletic and academic achievements. But I started realizing that I went from temporal happiness to temporal happiness without any kind of long-standing fulfillment or peace. Winning an all-tournament award, qualifying for Nationals, acing a final exam or a class, earning a degree, getting the girlfriend I wanted, having a fun night out of partying—*all* were temporal highs that never lasted and always went away, which led to a longing for another form of fulfillment.

Although never considering myself a "religious" person at the time, I began listening more and more to my buddy Rob Carlson. We were best friends since the age of ten. Rob was raised in a Christian home, although he was by far the black sheep of his family. One by one his older sisters got "saved" by accepting Jesus Christ as their Savior and, growing up, you could always sense a deep and unique peace in his home. Rob as a teenager would have no part of Jesus and ran 1,000 miles in the other direction to the point where he did jail time while I was in college for, among other things, theft and drug dealing. But in jail, God finally grabbed a hold of Rob's heart and it was hard for the most hardened of spiritual hearts not to notice the change in Rob upon his release. Where chaos once ruled, a peace now settled inside of him. Rob pronounced himself a "born-again" believer. His proclamation scared me to death initially. My knowledge at the time of so-called born-again believers were the Jim and Tammy Faye Bakkers and the Jimmy Swaggarts—the fallen televangelists of the '80s as well as the hill people that drank rat poison and danced with rattlesnakes during church. Suffice it to say I thought Rob had become a nut. But oddly enough, he was the same guy with the same personality and sense of humor although now someone who aspired to live a holier and purer, more fulfilling life.

Partly because I grew up in a rather watered-down denomination, my "religious" or church experience from childhood was rather hollow. Once I started working on Sundays in high school, going to church resided nowhere near my radar from that point forward. But I do remain grateful to my parents for taking me to church as a child and laying the basic building blocks of Christianity in my mind. Rob's Christian conversion and witness, therefore, was not altogether a foreign concept to me. With that said, I really had no idea what being a Christian meant. Once I started listening and then talking to Rob about his experience, the pieces of the puzzle started to come together for me as I started to think back to a few prior encounters. A Christian teammate from my rookie year of playing rugby gave me rides to the gym, along with a couple of his able-bodied friends who helped us out at practice. They were pretty down to earth guys and, again, you could sense a peace within these guys. Like Rob, my buddy Dave Ford, whom I was suite mates with in college, grew up in a Christian home. Dave introduced me to my college girlfriend who was from his hometown. So

I spent time in his home over school breaks when I visited my girlfriend and stayed with her family. Much like in Rob's home, you could sense a peace in Dave's home, and this was long before I knew why.

But mostly, I remember hanging out on the main quad (center of campus) between classes on a beautiful spring day at U of I in 1993. While watching girls, soaking up the sun, and talking to the occasional classmate walking by, I noticed a guy coming toward me with what looked like a Bible. And I thought to myself, *Oh boy, here we go.* I acted polite as he engaged me in small talk before asking me if I was a Christian.

"Sure," I responded. "I grew up in church. I believe in God."

He then asked if I thought I'd go to heaven. "Yeah, man," I said nicely. "I'm a good person."

He then explained to me a person needed to be "born-again" to go to heaven, before opening up his Bible to John 3:3: "Jesus declared, 'I tell you the truth, no one can see the kingdom of God unless he is born again.'"

Wow. For the first time I saw, in black and white, the Bible stating you must be born again. Although I politely excused myself from that guy as fast as possible, that moment profoundly impacted me and eventually bore fruit a couple of years later.

In late fall of 1995, God really began to work on my heart and started to water many of those previously planted seeds. One night, Rob and I talked into the early morning hours and, as he sat on the couch, he looked at me and said through tear-filled eyes, "I don't know why Jesus loves me as much as He does, but I'm glad." At that moment, I saw the peace of God transcended in another human being for the first time and I decided I wanted that peace too. That Sunday I went to Rob's church, a lively and upbeat contemporary Christian service. Unlike anything I experienced growing up, the pastor talked about Christianity not being a "religion" but rather a personal relationship with Jesus Christ. At the end of the service, he asked those who didn't know Jesus as Lord and Savior to pray this simple prayer:

"Father, I know that I'm a sinner and my sins have separated me from you. Now I want to turn away from my past sinful life toward you. Please forgive me. I believe that your son Jesus Christ died for my sins, was resurrected from the dead, is alive, and hears my prayer. I invite Jesus into my heart to become the Lord of my life, to rule and reign in me from this day forward. In Jesus' name I pray, Amen."

And with that, I became a Christian. From a biblical point of view, nothing else is required to become a Christian other than what Romans 10:10–13 admonishes us to do, which is to confess with your mouth and, more importantly, believe in your heart that Jesus is Lord. I can't say the heavens opened or that I heard the voice of God. But I can tell you that I felt an underlying peace that I had never felt in my life. Unlike the temporal highs, fulfillments, and pleasures that I described earlier, this new peace filled a part of my heart that nothing had ever filled.

Still facing an uncertain future, my internship ended and no doors opened for me in the broadcast sports world. I sent my resume to small and midsized television channels all over the

Midwest, receiving nothing more than the occasional "we'll keep your resume on file" response. I didn't realize it at the time, but with the explosion of the cable sports media in the 1990s, local television sports departments became smaller and less relevant. I wasn't faring much better in my hunt for a print job either as newspapers and their sports departments also became dinosaurs in a mid–1990s era that saw the dawn of the Internet. I submitted my resume and portfolio of experience when a job opening popped up for a small town paper about 100 miles outside Chicago. The job started at only $16,000 a year to cover local high school sports but caught my attention nonetheless. I made the cut for the interview and knew I possessed all the qualifications. But when the two editors saw me, and my wheelchair, for the first time, I sensed any energy and hope for that position drained from the room. Never before or after that incident have I knowingly experienced prejudice against me in any form. But I knew from the body language, demeanor, and tone in the room that I had zero shot at that job. For the first time, I empathized with other minorities who talked about experiencing silent or covert discrimination.

But instead of letting bitterness settle in, I began realizing spiritually that a bigger plan was in place and God had my best interests in mind. If at any point I would have landed a fulltime journalism job at this transition stage of my life, the events of the next fifteen years would not have unfolded the way they did. For one thing, I would have had to sacrifice my rugby career, which I was willing to do at the time in order to pursue what I thought was my dream as a sportswriter. No small-town wheelchair rugby teams existed in places like Iowa and Indiana where I predominately applied for jobs, and the heavy weekend hours covering high school sports were not conducive to competing in rugby tournaments, also held on weekends.

But in late November, a door opened that would provide me with the best of both worlds. *The Daily Southtown*, a midsized paper covering the South Suburbs and South Side of Chicago gave me a part-time job as a correspondent or "stringer." Although the pay was minimal and only part-time, I loved doing the job description of covering high school sports as well as the small college scene. Among ideas of mine that became front page feature stories that I wrote were "Big-time Shadows: Basketball players at small colleges find recognition hard to come by." I also broke the story and ended up the beat writer on tiny Lewis University's men's volleyball program. Nobody else covered them at the time and they eventually made it all the way to the NCAA Final Four before losing to UCLA. The program flew under the radar as men's volleyball lacks mass popularity. But it was too difficult to ignore a school like Lewis with an enrollment of 5,800 competing against universities with more than 35,000 students like UCLA, Hawaii, Penn State, and BYU. Early in the season, the tip about this program on the rise came from my pastor, whose brother coached the team. By default, and because no senior writers wanted the assignment, Lewis became my beat. Unfortunately, by the time they made it to the Final Four, the word was out, drawing the attention of our Senior Editor who promptly took a rookie like me off the assignment and sent a senior writer out to Los Angeles to cover the Final Four, which the host UCLA squad won. Although Lewis's coach expressed frustration over my demotion because I brought them into the media spotlight, I understood a pecking order exists in sports, as well as sports journalism, and one needs to pay their dues to get the trophy assignments. That said, I appreciated my experience at the *Southtown* which allowed me the flexibility to continue my true fulltime passion and focus on rugby as, at twenty-four, I began to peak physically.

I returned to play for Chicago, where I began as a rookie four seasons earlier, for my fifth year during the 1995–96 season. During that season, the United States Olympic Committee announced wheelchair rugby would be a Paralympic sport for the first time during the upcoming 1996 summer games in Atlanta. Tryouts would be held at the Olympic Training Center in Colorado Springs the week after Nationals in April. The United States Quad Rugby Association (USQRA) selected National teams in the past for international competitions, but this would be the first time our sport would be showcased at the highest level of wheelchair sports: the Paralympics.

At the time, I simply hoped to be one of the forty-two athletes given an invitation to the tryouts. I had never been selected to try out before, and to be picked out of the 300 or so players from around the country would be an honor—but also provide validation of my arrival as a player. I became disappointed, although not too surprised, when the invitations went out and my team wasn't notified of my inclusion on the tryout list. Still relatively unknown, particularly outside the Midwest, and with only six players from each of the seven classifications (.5, 1, 1.5, 2, 2.5, 3.0, 3.5) selected to tryout, I figured my chances were slim. I knew from my high school baseball experience that tryouts were a numbers game against tough competition. Still, I asked our regional representative to inquire as to whether or not an oversight had been made. To my surprise, he came back and told me that my invitation had been sent to my old University of Illinois address—that the committee indeed selected me to tryout. The funny thing was if I failed to inquire, the deadline for turning in the paperwork for the tryout would have come and gone with the selection committee giving my tryout opportunity to the next 1.5 on the list.

Our Chicago team qualified for Nationals that year for the first time since 1988 and finished seventh in the country—to this day the highest ever finish for Chicago, equaling their 2007 finish. The next week I flew out to Colorado Springs for a once in a lifetime opportunity. I remember arriving in the gym at the Olympic Training Center and truly just being happy to be there. I had no illusions of making the team and sat in awe as I looked at the other forty-one players, thinking to myself how great these guys were and what a privilege it was to be among them. The tryouts started on Thursday afternoon and continued until midday Sunday when they would announce the eight-man team.

As a 1.5, I not only competed against the other 1.5s, I competed against the 1.0s and 2.0s as well. I felt early in the tryouts that I separated myself as the best 1.5 and my confidence grew. But even so, there were no guarantees a 1.5 would be selected. The Gold

Medal winning national team at World Championships the year before included zero 1.5s on a twelve-man squad. The Paralympic National team, by contrast, would be comprised of only eight players. For selection, a 1.5 needed to play head and shoulders above the 1.0s and better than some of the 2.0s. The first day or so consisted primarily of drills with the coaches scoring you on your passing, catching, picking (blocking), and ball-handling abilities as well as timing you on speed and quickness drills. While nobody made the team based on how they drilled, the coaches certainly weeded guys out based on lack of endurance or speed or generally if they proved unable to keep up with the pack.

The more the tryout progressed, the more I felt my prospects increased to make the team. I remember vividly being grouped with the 1.5s on Friday night and one of the guys saying he didn't think the staff would pick any 1.5s. Right there, I remember a belief setting in that I was going to make it. Then a Christian for only a few months, I started praying that, win or lose, God would help me to perform to the best of my ability, and God delivered as I felt His power flowing through me the entire weekend. After going from 9:00 a.m.–8:00 p.m. on Friday, the first cut list was posted an hour or so later. Although technically nobody had been cut, clearly we saw from the two lists that the staff created an A group (twenty-four-man list) and B group (eighteen-man list). I found my name on the A group list—the only 1.5 still alive.

I continued playing well on Saturday and that night the staff made official cuts, posting a list of sixteen picked to continue playing on Sunday morning. From there, the coaches would pick the final eight-man team during lunch. A nervous anxiety gave way to relief and hope when I saw my name on that list. I remember Joe Soares, a 3.5 from Tampa and at the time the best player in the world, telling me that, no matter the outcome, what a great accomplishment it was to be among the final sixteen. As much as I agreed with him, I also knew nobody would remember or care whether I finished number nine or number forty-two at tryouts—the only thing people would remember was the final eight competing on the first Team USA for wheelchair rugby at Paralympics.

On Sunday morning, I got up and rolled down the hill to the cafeteria and just looked in awe at how beautiful the mountains looked with the sun glistening off the snow-capped mountain tops. I bulked up on a big breakfast, as the food at the Olympic Training Center was better than any you'll ever have anywhere else. The full menus ranged from made-to-order omelets for breakfast to porterhouse and sirloin steaks for dinner as well as a full ice cream and desert bar, all provided by USOC funding. As I settled in my rugby chair and warmed-up, I felt physically, spiritually, and mentally as strong as I ever felt before or since playing rugby. Once again I prayed that God would elevate me to the highest of my abilities. Sunday morning was all about scrimmaging, with the coaches gauging how you worked with different lineups. They grouped me with three different combinations. Down to the final sixteen, all the players and lines were strong, with no weak links left. I needed to muster every bit of energy, talent, desire, and drive inside of me. Feeling at the very top of my game and flat out in the zone, my speed was top notch and my passing crisp, with my blocking as good as my defense effective. Those three hours were the three best hours of rugby I ever played. At noon, the coaches dismissed us for lunch after which they'd announce the final team.

As we filtered back into the gym, a peace settled in over me. If nothing else, I had given all I had and completely emptied myself, which is all anybody can ever ask of themselves or others. Win, lose, or draw, always go out and maximize your potential. Ultimately, in any endeavor, be it your relationship with the Lord, your marriage, family, or your career, always give one hundred percent of yourself so no regrets are left when you finish. Terry Vinyard was the National team coach, the same coach from Tampa who noticed me at a tournament a year earlier when I was still an unknown. He rattled off the names of the players:

- **3.5** Joe Soares, Tampa—who many saw as a lock to make the team although he needed to play big on Sunday to clinch his spot as the coaches considered taking two 3.0s as opposed to a 3.5

- **3.0** Brad Updegrove, Houston—the fastest player in the world

- **2.5** Mike Wyatt, San Diego—who out-battled two 2.5s from his club team to win his spot

- **2.0** Dave Gould, Tampa—a pre-tryout lock to make the team as the best all around player in the world

- **2.0** Cliff Chunn, Tennessee—an up and coming eighteen-year-old on his way to becoming the best player in the world

And so Terry came to the sixth of eight spots. I hung onto his every word, unable to breath, as he commented that a lot of talk and questions revolved around whether or not they'd take a 1.5. He then said my performance made it impossible for them to cut me and introduced me as a member of the National team. At twenty-four years old, seven years removed from being unable to feed myself, that moment became the pinnacle of my life at the time and a prelude to every good thing that would come afterward. He then introduced the remaining two players:

- **1.0** Dave Ceruti, Connecticut—a guy who would move to Tampa the following year and someone I'd become very close with along with Soares and Gould in the following years

- **.5** Eddie Crouch, Tennessee—a perennial national teamer for over a decade through the 2004 Paralympics in Athens

These were the seven guys, along with Vinyard and his assistant Reggie Richer, who I spent a lot of time coming together and bonding with over the next six months, culminating with the 1996 Summer Paralympics in Atlanta. That summer, for a variety of reasons, would be the best summer of my life and the last before my full transition into adulthood became complete.

Aside from the build-up for the Paralympics which consisted of training camps in Toronto, Tampa, and San Antonio, the summer of '96 holds a special place in my heart. That summer was the last I lived at home and hence the last time my parents, my two brothers, and I lived under the same roof. My home always provided a safe place for me growing up and always a place where I felt loved as well as welcomed. Years went by before I realized the summer of '96 was the last true care-free summer for me, and the blessings I enjoyed growing up in the home I did with the parents and brothers I'd been given.

I returned home after tryouts with the momentum beginning to build around town for me as a member of Team USA. I was interviewed and featured in both the print and broadcast media, capped with the Fox affiliate in Chicago doing a feature on me for their Sunday night sports show. I had photo shoots and sponsors lining up during this glorious time. Staying humble, I began growing as a Christian by immersing myself more in church and reading my Bible every day, ultimately realizing none of this was about me or my doing. All of this culminated with my baptism in July. I realized I was blessed and would keep things in their proper perspective. Although not setting out to memorize scripture at that time, a verse kept sticking in my mind. James 1:4 became my signature verse: "Perseverance must finish its work so that you may be mature and complete, not lacking anything." I came to see sports, as well as life, as a test of faith and endurance with the ultimate winners persevering while becoming mature and complete as athletes, spouses, parents, employees, and citizens.

Another door opened for me that summer when approached by fellow National teamer Joe Soares about moving to Tampa. Ever since that day looking out my parent's window at the snow during my first winter in a wheelchair, I desired to move to a warm weather climate while continually growing weary of Chicago winters. The previous winter before Paralympics, our Chicago team played at a tourney in Tennessee and at the airport afterward we were in the same wing as the Tampa and San Diego teams. With both returning to warm weather climates, we headed back to

Chicago where a fifteen-degree temperature awaited us. I envied those Tampa and San Diego guys. My decision was clinched—I was moving somewhere warm; so I listened intently when Soares approached me. He told me I could spend a month with his family in Tampa, where we'd train in addition to him helping me to find a job and a place to live. Taking him up on his offer, I stayed with Joe in July and found employment counseling at a Center for Independent Living for people with disabilities. The job began in September once I moved down. By this time, I realized that my future lay not in either print or broadcast journalism so I relied more on my undergraduate education. No fulltime opportunities were available at the *Daily Southtown*, where I had been working, and the few fulltime jobs that presented themselves consisted of covering high school football in corn fields for $16,000 a year— not exactly my calling especially when I needed flexibility to commit to rugby, which was a fulltime job all by itself.

I stayed in Tampa from mid July through the first week of August, returning home to finish preparation for the Paralympics, which took place from August 15–25. Our national team truly came together on the court and off through our various training camps, and, for the first time in my life, I was about to experience being part of a dynasty unlike any my sport had ever seen: The United States Quad Rugby National Team. At the same time, a dynasty was at its peak in Chicago.

CHAPTER 9

The Last Great Dynasty

When I started following sports in the late 1970s and on into the early '80s, Chicago was a graveyard for professional basketball with the Bulls ranging from bad to mediocre. You couldn't give Bulls tickets away in an era when the DePaul Blue Demons dominated market share amongst Chicago area basketball fans as well as receiving the bulk of the media attention. All of this changed in the summer of 1984. DePaul coach Ray Meyer retired the previous March and the Bulls drafted Michael Jordan with the third overall pick in June. Jordan, well-known coming out of North Carolina, was the best player that summer on the '84 Gold medal winning Olympic team, a squad so talented that future Hall of Famer Charles Barkley got cut from the final roster. So everyone knew the Bulls had something big in Michael Jordan but no one could know just how big he or the Bulls would become over the next fifteen years.

Like Walter Payton in his early years, the Bulls with Jordan personified a one-man gang. And like Payton's Bears, the Bulls finished each season with average results until the organization brought in other quality players to compliment Jordan. Years later, Bulls general manager Jerry Krause took a lot of heat from the players and in the media for saying "organizations" and not players "win championships." The reality though is that he was right. Neither the Bulls nor the Bears became a contender and then a champion without successful people around Jordan or Payton. The parallels from these athletes extend to my life. The successful transition I made after my injury and the subsequent development of the drive to succeed academically directly resulted from the support of my parents, brothers, extended family, and closest friends. My growth as an athlete, the individual accolades, and team accomplishments became reality with great teammates and coaches around me. And eventually, my growth and success as a Christian, husband, father, and businessman reached levels beyond my initial comprehension with a wide network of successful role models, advisors, and confidants. So if you want to attain success, first surround yourself with equally driven, talented people. Bulls' management also provided lessons by not engaging in a popularity contest and not worrying about what the media would write. They made tough choices that proved correct even though many seemed unpopular at the time.

In Jordan's first four years, he became the most electrifying player in the NBA and the Bulls began their ascent into the national sporting discussion. But the team was mediocre, having won only a single playoff game in Jordan's first three years. The questions began to surface on whether Michael played too much like an individual player in a team sport, whether he possessed the ability to make his team better, and ultimately whether the Bulls or Jordan could win a championship. A *Sports Illustrated* cover story in March of 1989 addressed these very issues, but all those questions changed once the 1989 NBA playoffs began in late April.

The Renje Boys circa 1981

The Renje Boys circa 1985—you can see I was never shy in displaying my Chicago sports roots

The Renje Boys circa 1989

1996 Summer Paralympics in Atlanta, Georgia

Meeting President Bill Clinton

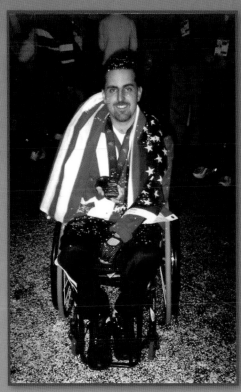

Gold medal, 2000 Summer Paralympics in Sydney, Australia

My #1 fan and life partner

Medal Stand at the 2000 Summer Paralympics

Celebrating winning gold

Amy and Bill in 2010

My three most precious gifts

Two years earlier, Bulls general manager Jerry Krause pulled off one of the most defining if not greatest drafts in NBA history. With two picks in the top ten, he traded up (from the eighth to fifth pick) for an unknown player named Scottie Pippen. Pippen was a true American fairy tale. He grew up the youngest of twelve children in rural Arkansas and wasn't offered a single college scholarship, not even to a junior college. He "walked on" as a non-scholarship player to a small school where he literally worked as a locker room towel boy his freshman year. But he grew six inches before his sophomore year and started developing as a basketball player. Pippen was soon after discovered by Krause, who drafted him and then selected Horace Grant at number ten. And with that draft, the nucleus for an NBA dynasty was born.

The Bulls entered the playoffs with a 47–35 record and the sixth seed. They went in as heavy underdogs against a young, talented, and well-balanced Cleveland Cavalier team who were the number three seed while finishing the regular season ten games better than the Bulls. Most "experts" predicted a sweep, mostly because the Bulls lost all six games against the Cavs in the regular season. But in what would become a vintage Jordan tactic, he used the perceived slight from the media to motivate both himself and his team. In an era of white sneakers, the Bulls decided to wear all black shoes for the playoffs in a symbol of team unity. When the Bulls upset Cleveland in Game 1 of the Best of Five series, they set the tone for the defining series of the Jordan era.

The teams traded wins, but when the Bulls (up two games to one) fell short at home in overtime in Game 4, Cleveland looked like they would prevail with Game 5 on their home court. Jordan blamed himself for the loss after missing free throws late in the game. Jordan's personal accountability in accepting responsibility also proved to be the mark of a champion while he vowed to make amends in Game 5. Lots of good and even great athletes and teams make these types of proclamations, but few follow through to delivery. Champions are born during these moments. From a team and individual standpoint, Jordan and the Bulls needed a signature win to build on if they would eventually hope to become champions. Game 5 in Cleveland provided that moment.

In a wild game with a crazed Cleveland crowd on their feet for what seemed like most of the second half, the lead changed hands multiple times—including three times in the last ten seconds. A Jordan jump shot put the Bulls up 99–98 with 6.6 seconds left. But joy quickly dissipated for the Bulls while the Cleveland crowd erupted again as Craig Ehlo quickly scored a lay-up off a give and go after a timeout to put Cleveland up one with 3.5 seconds left. Larry Bird once said in a tie game that all five guys want to take the last shot; but if a team is down one, maybe one guy wants to take the shot with the other four hoping the ball doesn't find a way into their hands. Michael Jordan always wanted and demanded to take the last shot. After an immediate timeout, the Bulls inbounded at half court with Jordan frantically fighting through screens trying to free himself for the inbounds pass. Eluding two defenders, Jordan took the inbounds pass, quickly dribbled to the top of the key, and jumped. Ehlo played great defense and managed to stay right with Jordan. He actually leaped at the same time as Jordan; but Jordan, living up to his Air Jordan nickname, stayed elevated longer. As Ehlo cleared, Jordan, now on his way down but still in the air, got his shot off, which rattled around and went in at the buzzer—game over, series over. The arena went funeral parlor quiet as the stunned crowd stood in disbelief while the Bulls celebrated wildly.

That play, known now in both cities as "The Shot" became the defining moment for both teams. The Cavs, who Magic Johnson said earlier that season would become the team of the 1990s, would be eliminated by the Bulls in the playoffs three more times in 1992, '93, and '94 when their window of opportunity finally slammed shut. Meanwhile, the Bulls eventually became the team of the 1990s, later pointing to this game as giving them the confidence to achieve every accomplishment that would come afterward. Aside from Jordan, Pippen and Grant came of age, maturing during that series, and Center Bill Cartwright justified Jerry Krause's vilified trade the year before with his tough defense on the Cavs' All-Star center, the younger and more-talented Brad Daugherty. Cartwright continued this trend over the next five years, playing against and neutralizing more talented centers, like the Knicks' Patrick Ewing.

In the next round of the '89 playoffs, the Bulls again pulled off an upset by beating the second-seeded Knicks in six games. The conference finals next, they took a 2–1 series lead before dropping three in a row to the Detroit Pistons. The Pistons were the best team in basketball with their only two playoff losses coming to the Bulls. Detroit would win the NBA Championship in 1989 and again in '90 while providing the last psychological hurdle for the Bulls—a daunting task as they eliminated the Bulls in the '88, '89, and '90 seasons. No matter though; the Bulls were coming, and you could sense it was only a matter of time before they would break through the Pistons.

After the 1989 season, the Bulls' front office made an unpopular move with the fans as well as the media, but a move eventually and overwhelmingly proved correct. Doug Collins was the popular head coach and, in his three years, the Bulls improved each season, culminating with the '89 playoff run. But in June, the Bulls shockingly fired Collins and replaced him with an unknown assistant named Phil Jackson. Bulls owner Jerry Reinsdorf and his GM Krause (who hired Jackson as an NBA assistant when no opportunities existed for him in the league) took a tremendous amount of heat. But Jackson, through a blend of coaching and personal philosophies, proved to be a steady hand in guiding the Bulls. Through assistant coach Tex Winter, he implemented the Triangle Offense which forces passing among the players on the court and ball distribution to get all five guys involved in the flow of the offense. Jackson properly harnessed the talent and energy of a great individual player like Jordan, not an easy task with a player of MJ's caliber. Jackson helped him to fully comprehend true sacrifice and giving of one's self. Credit goes to Jordan for reinventing himself by understanding and having the willingness to change his mindset for the betterment of his team. The Bulls inched closer in the 1989–90 season and pushed the Pistons to the brink in the Eastern Conference Finals before losing the series four games to three.

During the 1990–91 season, the Bulls faced the Pistons in the playoffs for the fourth time in a row and the third time consecutively in the conference finals. A tremendous amount of mental strength is required to overcome an opponent after years of tough losses. And to say the Pistons were in the Bulls' heads was an understatement. Detroit's nickname was the "Bad Boys" due to a reputation for pushing their opponents around, with the Bulls as no exception. But by then, the Bulls endured all the tough losses, taking those experiences to persevere while growing stronger as a unit. They were ready to take the next step and dominated the Pistons in a four-game sweep. With their final hurdle cleared, no team could stop the Bulls. They became only the third team in NBA history to win three straight NBA titles from 1991 through 1993. And after Jordan came back from an almost two-season sabbatical, they again won three straight from 1996–98.

The snapshot from the first title etched into the history of Chicago fans and the NBA was Jordan cradling the trophy in tears. In that picture we see illuminated the lost value in sport of delayed gratification. Jordan, unlike his contemporaries like Bird or Magic, waited for seven years while often enduring some inferior teams early in his career (see Walter Payton) before finally winning a professional championship. The struggle and all the perseverance came gushing out in his tears. This championship, as the Bears' Super Bowl, took three years with the core of that team, three years of making strides before finally accomplishing the ultimate goal. I appreciate those championships as a fan because I grew and endured with those teams, hoping, dreaming, yet wondering along the way if they'd ever get there. Nowadays, the fans, media and sports organizations themselves want to win immediately and show no patience for the values of growing and coming together over time.

The Bulls became the only professional sports team in my lifetime to win six championships in eight years. And with the structure of sports in the modern era—team salary caps and free agency—we're unlikely to ever see another championship run like the 1990s Bulls' again. In thirteen seasons, Michael Jordan's Bulls team *never* lost a playoff series they were supposed to win and won five as the underdog. In a city with so many prior sporting collapses and disappointments, this feat to me is the most understated. It's a feat that no other athlete in my lifetime can lay claim to—not any of Jordan's contemporaries like Bird or Magic or anybody from the current era such as Kobe or Lebron.

Looking back, I miss the old Chicago Stadium almost as much as the Bulls or Blackhawks teams from that period. The Stadium was considered the loudest indoor arena in North America. Built in 1929 and constructed with a close-quartered layout, the seats sat almost right on top of the playing surface. Building codes today prevent such a tight-knit construction. The Bulls were the first team that dimmed the house lights for a "spotlight" introduction. With The Alan Parsons Project's "Eye in the Sky" blaring over the loud speakers, the spotlight panned the crowd, capturing the championship banners as well as the individual players upon introduction. With a flashing Bulls logo displayed on the scoreboard, the crowd erupted as soon as the lights dimmed and grew steadily louder as Public Address announcer Ray Clay bellowed out "And now, the starting lineups for your World Champion Chicago Bulls!" By the time each of the four starters were introduced, he peaked with "From North Carolina ..." and you couldn't hear anything but the roar of the crowd as Michael

Jordan was introduced as the fifth and final starter. The Stadium just added to the Bulls' mystique in those days.

But for me, the best thing about the Chicago Stadium was actually the inaccessibility to wheelchair users. Constructed long before disability awareness, no elevators resided in the stadium. So I routinely bought standing-room tickets ($25 for playoff games) and sat right on the main floor, just feet away from the court and the Bulls bench as opposed to up in the nosebleed seats with the rest of the standing-room only crowd. From my injury in 1989 until progress in the form of a wrecking ball tore the stadium down in '94, I went to dozens of Bulls (and Blackhawk) games while enjoying all the perks of sitting floor-level for the price of a standing-room only ticket. I shook hands with and met Chicago Bear players of that era. I also met Jack Nicholson before Game 7 of the '92 conference semifinals against the Knicks as he took in a game during the filming of the movie *Hoffa*.

Above all, my favorite Chicago Stadium memory and that of a life-long Chicago fan was sitting on the floor (and being seen on TV) for Game 6 of the 1992 Finals against Portland. The Bulls, up 3 games to 2, found themselves down by fifteen going into the fourth quarter. In one of many master moves made by Phil Jackson over the course of his career, he started the final quarter with four bench players to go along with Scottie Pippen. Jackson, always recognizing the value of "the tribe" above all, would later say the Bulls needed fresh energy on the court. With primarily role players, the Bulls cut the deficit to five—all happening with Jordan on the bench. The crowd, in an absolute frenzy, saw Jordan return to the game fresh and well rested, while knowing Portland had no chance. Two Jordan free throws with twelve seconds left gave the Bulls a 97–93 lead and sealed the win. I vividly remember watching the clock run down to zero and the ensuing euphoria as the team ran off the court in celebration before returning to salute the fans. Nobody left or stopped cheering for probably the next thirty minutes as an endless loop of Gary Glitter's "Rock and Roll Part 2" and Queen's "We Will Rock You/We Are the Champions" saturated the stadium.

Afterward, we hit Rush Street with the party in full swing. I rolled down the street and just high-fived people who were driving by in their cars with horns honking all over. The city was electric and alive. Although I moved from the Chicago Area to Tampa in the mid '90s for warmer weather, my heart never left nor did I ever stop loving or following the teams of my youth. Many different levels of fandom exist, from the casual fan to the diehard. But I've never understood how someone could be a true fan without growing up or at least living in that team's area for a long period of time. I think you need to experience the collective civic euphoria when your team wins as well as the heartache that falls upon the entire city when your team loses to be a true fan. Nothing was more exciting for me than the buzz and vibe in and around Chicago when a winning team is in town. Everywhere you go, people talked about it—every media outlet (print and broadcast) covered it as the lead story, every store window and street corner had apparel for sale. This full-blown immersion of the sporting culture seeps into you and inevitably is how a fan is cultivated. Living in Tampa, I miss not being around Chicago for those title runs. By the Bulls' fifth championship in 1997, I lived in Tampa and might as well have lived on another planet. I took a date with me into a sports bar to watch one of the championship games and the place sat almost empty—nobody cared; no buzz for the Bulls existed.

As for my memories of Jordan, I actually got a chance to meet him three days after they won the title. One of my rugby teammates and I finished working out at the Rehab Institute of Chicago, located half a mile from the CBS studios where Jordan was filming a post-championship wrap-up show. So we headed down there and found probably a couple of hundred people who gathered on both sides of the sidewalk hoping to get a glimpse of Michael. We did better than that as we pulled a page from the Bobby Brady playbook in the "Joe Namath" episode of The Brady Bunch by explaining to the guard that we only "had six months to live." The guard didn't buy our story and neither did a CBS executive who walked in simultaneously. But he admired our tenacity and ushered us in where we watched the end of the show's taping. Afterward, he introduced us to Jordan, whom we shook hands with and spoke to for a few minutes. I'm sure this moment provided a career highlight for Michael as well and I look forward to reading about it in his autobiography someday.

So many things set Michael apart that I've learned to emulate in the arena of athletics and life. Yes, he benefited from more God-given talent than most. But he built, trained, and worked upon that talent to go from a great player to another level without an adjective to adequately explain that level. Michael always looked for an edge to improve himself, be it a slight from an opponent, the media, or an opposing coach. Cut from the varsity high school team as a sophomore, and really ever since then, he carried around an "I'll prove you wrong" chip on the shoulder as evidenced in his classic Hall of Fame induction speech. Late in his career, when he lacked the explosiveness to drive to the basket, he improvised and worked to develop a fade-away jump shot, illustrating again how important it is to always try to improve yourself, even after you've tasted success, in order to maintain that level. And lastly, in a team sport, he recognized the value and need to have great people around him and bought into a system preached by Jackson—a system that emphasized the whole or sum of the parts as opposed to the individual.

CHAPTER 10

Golden Era

Our Paralympic team arrived in Atlanta and after processing, we were driven to the Olympic Village. The Paralympics are held within weeks after the Olympics and in all the same venues. Everything, and I mean everything, is top notch. They give you credentials during processing to wear around your neck which pretty much gives you a license to do and go wherever you want. The Olympic Village, which you couldn't get into without your credentials, was like a highly secured small town. The Village included dorms housing the athletes, a training center, a large cafeteria with a full menu of meals, a venue with music entertainment every night, round the clock transportation to the various athletic venues (and Downtown Atlanta), and a town center where you could even go get a haircut if you wanted. Again, everything was free, even the vending machines. They gave you a card to access any vending machine in any venue—if you were a Paralympic athlete, you wanted for nothing, as all your needs were met.

The best moment off the court was the night of Opening ceremonies. Atlanta built an Olympic Stadium (now Turner Field) just for the Olympics. As we lined up next door at the stadium the Atlanta Braves baseball team formerly played in, I sat convinced we would be marching into an empty Olympic Stadium with a few scattered friends and family cheering us on. I even remarked to Joe Soares that only a thousand people would be in the stands. But as we lined up next door a couple of hours prior, I saw a continuous stream of people entering the stadium and they just kept coming. As the host country, we came out of the tunnel and entered the stadium last, so the anticipation and excitement continued to build as a calm, summer night fell over Atlanta.

The most exhilaration I ever felt was coming through the stadium underneath where all the entertainers performing during the ceremonies lined up to cheer for us as we passed through the tunnel. As we made our way through those tunnels, my hair stood up on my arms hearing the performers chanting "USA, USA, USA" extremely loud, drowning out all other noise and preventing us from even hearing the guy next to us. More of the same awaited us coming out of a tunnel to a few more people than I originally thought—65,000! To hear that many people chanting for you and to see all those light bulbs flashing with thousands of pictures taken of us provided a scene I will never forget.

The rugby tournament didn't start until the following week. So Week 1 was spent with training in the morning, then sight-seeing as well as watching other events such as track and field during the afternoon and evenings. We soaked up the feeling of being big-time athletes around town while we realized the small window of fame would only last as long as the two-week Paralympics. In Team USA gear 24/7 and with all the awareness from the local media, everybody knew who we were and wanted to get as close to us as possible. We couldn't go anywhere without being asked for autographs or to have our pictures taken, and there were daily media interviews, all of which gave us a definitive once in a lifetime experience.

Once the rugby tournament began, we certainly experienced no letup in the frenzied aura and atmosphere. Along with Team USA, the tournament field included the following qualifying national teams: Canada (also from the Western Zonal), Great Britain (European Zonal), Sweden (European Zonal), Australia (Eastern Zonal), and New Zealand (Eastern Zonal). While our club team tournaments are held in rather unassuming venues and played in front of family and friends, Paralympic rugby is played in state of the art facilities with all the ambiance of a college or professional game, complete with a high tech sound system. My parents, brothers, grandma, Uncle Bob, Aunt Barb, and their kids all came to see me play, continuing a tradition of family support always given to me, in particular with my athletic endeavors.

On the court, we were the heavy favorite as Canada was really the only competitor for us back in the mid '90s. And as everyone thought, we ended up playing Canada for the Gold Medal. An electric atmosphere awaited us in the gym at Atlanta Metropolitan College with, at that time, a record attendance of 7,500 (which would be bested in Sydney 2000 by sellouts of 15,000). The gym was small and loud as chants of "USA, USA" greeted the introductions.

Our previous four games were all blowouts and not in question after the first quarter. The veteran Canadian team, however, would not be a willing participant to our gold coronation before the largely American crowd. They came out extremely tough; but our patience, poise, and depth ultimately wore them down. My only goal came with about four minutes to go as the game was getting out of reach for the Canadians. We were holding a four-goal lead and Soares forced a Canadian turnover near their goal-line as they were getting ready to score. As he fought for the ball, I broke for our goal at the opposite end. Soares came up with the ball, spotted me, and threw it my way. I remember the roar of the crowd getting louder and louder as his pass sailed in the air, making its way toward me with a perfect arc. I also remember thinking, *Man, I better not drop this pass.* No chance that was going to happen, as the pass hit me in full stride. I clutched it and out-paced the Canadian chasing me and after I crossed the goal-line, Canada called their last timeout. The crowd stood as one on their feet, and we embraced on the sideline with "The Macarena" blaring from the sound system.

A few minutes later, the final buzzer sounded and we were Gold Medalists with a 37–30 victory. Seemingly the crowd never stopped their ovation and before we hit the locker room to prepare for the medal ceremony, we took a victory lap around the court to embrace and high-five our families, friends, and fans. Once they hung those gold medals around our necks and played the National Anthem, all of our preparation as a team and a long personal journey for me was complete. I would often reflect back over the next few months on James 1:4, my signature verse, and think about how in seven years I had gone from a broken man to a Paralympic Gold Medalist.

Two days later on my flight back to Chicago, I was asked for another autograph. Our assistant coach, also on that flight, told me to enjoy the moment because that would probably be the last autograph I'd give. And he was partially right—the next autograph I gave came four years later in Sydney, Australia. My experience in, and leading up to, Atlanta was the pinnacle of my athletic career and an experience that the Lord would use to lay the foundation for future success in athletics, as well as in life, business, and marriage.

I returned to Tinley Park after the 1996 Paralympics with a Gold Medal around my neck and a hero's welcome awaiting me. My parents hosted a party for me also serving as a send off with my upcoming move to Tampa. In retrospect, I wish I had spent more time then relishing my last summer with my family in the home where I spent my formative years. Although a bright future lay ahead of me, you can never get back your youth and I do miss the times of intimacy and closeness provided by my mom, dad, and brothers in the twenty-five years I spent with them. At that point though, I excitedly headed for Florida with all my possessions at the time: a twin bed, desk, dresser, stereo, and clothes. I set out for Tampa knowing that the only time I'd be coming back "home" would be as a visitor. One of my old U of I teammates, Norm Lyduch, made the move with me, and we lived together for the next three years.

Not much time passed before I settled in and felt comfortable in Tampa. I arrived in early September so I only suffered through the remainder, a month and a half, of the Florida summer before experiencing the Florida winter. After living the last seven years in a wheelchair in the Midwest, Tampa winters were paradise. I never felt too limited by my wheelchair living in Illinois except during the winter. Growing up, I always enjoyed snowball fights, sledding, making forts, and playing football in the snow. But to reiterate, winter and wheelchairs don't mix. Now, I lived in a climate where I could eat in an outdoor café on the beach and watch the sunset in January. Definitely feeling at home, I gained a growing network of friends, first through rugby, then work, and ultimately Idlewild Baptist Church.

Rugby opened up the door for me to move to Florida, and playing for the Tampa Generals helped take my game to another level. The Generals won the national title in 1992, '93, and '95 and were coached by National Team coach Terry Vinyard. Further, the team's two stars, 3.5 Joe Soares and 2.0 Dave Gould, also played for the National team. Unfortunately from a team perspective, Norm (a Class 1.0) and I, along with another Class 1.0 fellow national teamer Dave Ceruti, arrived after the end of their championship run. Other teams began to catch up to the Generals before we arrived. While deep in low pointers (.5s to 1.5s), our team lacked another dominant high-point player to compliment Soares or at least back him up. Sharp Shadow (San Diego) beat Tampa for the national title in 1996, the year before we arrived, and would win again in '97 and '98. Eventually Lakeshore (Birmingham) would supplant Shadow by winning six straight titles beginning in 1999. Both those teams began to develop as well as recruit dominant mid and high-point players from other nearby teams. By 1998, the three best 2.5s in the country played for Shadow.

We remained a contender, however, through the rest of the decade, finishing third in 1997 (Spokane Nationals) and again in 1998 (Salt Lake City Nationals) after two heartbreaking losses in the National Semifinal each year. We finished fourth in 2000 while playing without Gould, who missed most of the season with a shoulder injury that would then end his career. Going in with the fifth seed, we upset our old nemesis and number two seed Sharp Shadow in the quarterfinals. To me, I took more pride in our fourth place finish as opposed to third the previous two seasons because of what we overcame as a team that year, fighting through a career-ending injury to the backbone of our team. The year 2000 would also be the peak of my career individually as I stepped into the number two position (behind Soares) vacated by Gould. Playing a number two role as a 1.5 for a team that finished top four in the nation was no small feat and something not done before or since. For my efforts, I won the USQRA Athlete of the Year award after the season and was told by then National team head coach Reggie Richner that no other player in the country played higher above his classification that season than I did.

I knew nothing of being nominated for, or winning, the award until the banquet held on Sunday night after the conclusion of Nationals in Louisville. My head coach Terry Vinyard, fiancée Amy, and parents all knew the week prior but conspired in keeping it quiet from me. Amy, who I'd been engaged to for three months, and my parents told me they wanted to see me compete in my last Nationals so they'd be coming to watch. I previously had announced I was retiring after the 2000 Sydney games to be held that October. Our team scheduled to fly out Sunday afternoon but Terry told me that he needed me to stay and represent the team that night at the banquet with him, and thus I'd have an extra evening to spend with my parents who flew in from Chicago. I sat there at the table when Terry went up to the podium to, I thought, announce the induction of a former player into the Hall of Fame. As he continued his speech, however, I realized he was describing me. Shocked, I went up to accept the award once he made the announcement. That moment certainly was a great memory to be able to share with my parents and soon-to-be wife.

Winning the Athlete of the Year award and becoming a perennial National Team member would not have been possible without making the move to Tampa in 1996. Looking back now, I would likely have been a one-hit wonder by staying in Chicago. Although already a member of Team USA, playing in the Generals gym with a coach and other players with long, impressive rugby résumés took my game to a whole new level. A fine line exists between confidence and arrogance. Arrogance is when you underestimate and don't give proper respect to a worthy opponent. Arrogance is thinking that you're the reason for your team's success. Confidence is when you think you're better than your opponent but you realize their value and know you need to bring your best performance or you may get beaten. Confidence, as an individual playing a team sport, is understanding your role as well as the value of your teammates and how a team functions as a single unit. And again, these lessons carry over into personal relationships such as work and marriage.

One of the keys to maintaining success after you've achieved it is remaining humble by not falling in love with yourself, so to speak, yet remaining confident in your abilities. Too many athletes let success go to their head and are oblivious to what it takes to continue to win and achieve once they get to the top. The climb up the mountain is tough but more difficult to stay there with everybody trying to knock you off. Playing with the Tampa Generals kept me humble and challenged me to be even better.

I was twenty-five when I came to Tampa and probably cockier than I should've been when I told Terry Vinyard upon my arrival that "no one would work harder than me." I expected him to say something along the lines of "that's great and just the attitude we need." Instead, he kind of chuckled and said "Do you think you're going to work harder than Dave Gould?" And as we started the 1996–97 season in October, I began to realize just how hard those guys worked to get to and stay at an elite level. Practices were intense with heavy endurance drills and fast-paced scrimmaging, certainly more so than anything I experienced playing at Chicago and Illinois. Also longer, we practiced three hours (as opposed to two) twice a week and often times six hours (as opposed to three) on Saturdays. Off the court, Soares hand-cycled twenty miles a day and Gould had a full gym of workout equipment in his garage to supplement his on-court training. In an atmosphere like this, you either elevate your game or quit because you can't keep up. For his role, Vinyard was like a tough father or high school football coach—you hated him at times because of his ability to push your buttons. But if you allowed yourself to be led by him, he would always make you a better player. Vinyard ran off a few guys over the years. Usually, though, those that quit lacked the mental approach and drive to get the most out of their abilities.

Instead of plateauing after 1996, the atmosphere in and around the Generals gym helped take my individual game from being among the best low-pointers (.5 to 1.5) in the country to among the best in the world. I choose not to delude myself into thinking I was above reproach and looked around at those within the Generals program to make myself better. As such, I made the National team again in 1998 as we would travel to Toronto to compete against twelve other countries in the World Championships. My line started in the Gold Medal game against New Zealand in a tightly contested game that we won 31–28. For my efforts, my fellow participants named me to the All-World team after the Championships.

Our club team in Tampa was loaded with low-pointers so we started competing in low-point tournaments in the off season. While traditional rugby games allow eight total points on the court per team, low-point tournaments only allow 3.5 total points. Most teams don't have enough low-pointers or at least enough quality low-pointers to field a competitive team, so they'll combine with other teams. In my career, our Tampa team was the only homegrown, true low-point club team while we competed against teams made up of players from several different club teams.

The most prestigious low-point tournament is the Defi Sportif held every May in Montreal. For six years in a row, a team called the Cannibals won the Sportif with no team ever coming closer to them than ten goals. They were comprised of All-Star .5s and 1.0s from all over the U.S. At one point before I achieved national team notoriety, I approached them about playing with them. They told me they didn't want or need a 1.5, as they were confident running a 1.0, 1.0, 1.0, .5 line as opposed to a 1.5, 1, .5, .5 line. So that perceived slight fueled my fire as we entered the Defi Sportif in May 1997. Among other teams in the eight-team tourney were a Canadian team and a Swiss team, both loaded with low-pointers from their national team.

We beat Canada in the semi-final and were set to play the Cannibals in the title game broadcast in French-Canadian throughout Quebec. Terry Vinyard set-up a "triangle-and-one" defensive press with our two .5s at the bottom of the triangle located near the baseline to trap the in-bounder as he came onto the court. Our Class 1 set up shop at the top of the triangle located at the free throw line with the responsibility of forcing offensive players down into the .5s. My position was the "and-one" about 5 feet higher than the Class 1 at the three-point line. Basically, I roamed and guarded anybody up high. The Cannibals wore down throughout the course of the game, and after being tied at halftime, we pulled away and beat the team that no one had ever come within ten goals of by a score of 26–20. I was awarded the MVP and took part in my first post-game television interview.

By the summer of 1999, I had traveled and played all over the U.S., usually with Ceruti (Rudy), Gould (Goldie) and Soares as we spent a few extra days after Nationals to see the sites. A year before, the four of us hung around and went up into the mountains in Salt Lake City, which is just absolutely pristine. We also wandered around downtown and, in a scene reminiscent of my encounter with meeting Michael Jordan, a janitor let us into an empty Delta Center where the Utah Jazz play. We rolled onto the floor where I looked around and imagined what it felt like for the Bulls to play for a championship on that floor. I even posed with my shooting hand extended in the position where Jordan had sunk the shot to beat the Jazz in the "flu game" in the 1997 NBA Finals, which was the very spot from which he'd also hit the winning shot for the title two months later in June of '98, his last shot as a Bull.

In 1999 after Nationals in Phoenix, Rudy, Goldie, and I piled into a rental car and went on to Sedona, drove through the desert, and finally ended up at the Grand Canyon. For someone who grew up in Illinois and then lived in Florida, traveling out west was nothing short of breathtaking. Piling three or four guys in wheelchairs into a rental car always provided us with stories and experiences to share. Just getting into and out of the car was an adventure. As the driver, I'd get in first, and Rudy as the other low-pointer then transferred into the passenger side. Goldie put both our chairs into the trunk then transferred himself into the back seat then disassembled and pulled his chair in with him. When Soares traveled with us, he would be stuck with putting our chairs into the trunk since he was our most functional guy. The whole experience took about fifteen minutes. Able-bodied people, who tend to take daily life skills like getting into and out of a car for granted, often can't believe that we have to go through such a process. But really, what alternative do we have other than sitting at home and feeling sorry for ourselves? And the reality is we look forward to the challenge of completing tasks that able-bodied people take for granted. Further, we're thankful for the function to live and travel independently, as not everybody enjoys this luxury. One time I was getting into my car when I noticed a bus full of senior citizens staring at me in a collective trance with their noses pressed against the bus windows. When I got the chair into the car and shut the door, they actually started clapping! I'm sure I was the talk of their community at their next bingo night.

During our trip to the Grand Canyon, however, we did experience a bit of angst. We left Phoenix and set out on the six-hour drive to the Canyon with the trip through the mountains and desert being nothing short of incredible. Most of our drive seemed to be state and county roads as opposed to highway, which allowed us to really soak up the scenery. We booked a wheelchair-accessible room at the Canyon and, at a time before GPS and Yahoo Maps, took down directions on how to get there from a map provided by our hotel concierge in Phoenix. None of us had ever been to the Canyon so we just assumed you drive into town, check into your hotel, and then it's off to see the Canyon. Well, as dusk approached with our gas tank on E, we pulled up to the entrance and quickly figured out it was one of many entrances. Somehow, our directions took us to an obscure entryway. We drove miles without seeing anything—not a hotel, a restaurant, or a gas station. So we were happy to get there as we were hungry, needed gas, and were anxious to check into our hotel. All that changed as the woman in the booth proceeded to tell us our hotel was completely on the opposite end of the Canyon: six hours away by car!

So now we're forced to find a different hotel—not always an easy task because we need wheelchair accessibility. We also need gas quickly, as well as food. The woman in the booth didn't exactly have the gift of patience as we asked her to point us to a gas station. She replied "I have a line" and motioned to the cars lined up behind us. She provided no additional help and motioned us into the vast Canyon. We couldn't backtrack as it had been forty-five minutes or so since we last passed anything other than a cactus. So we trudged along, and while the winding, heavily wooded roadways are great for pleasant scenic drives, they're not very pleasant when you're four starving guys in wheelchairs without a hotel and about to run out of gas. The thought ran through all our heads that we were going to be forced to sleep in the stalled car until sunlight, when we'd be able to wave down some assistance. Eventually we found an exit and this time it led to a resort town where a much-needed gas station and a hotel with an accessible room awaited us. The next two days were spent just staring in awe at the craftsmanship of God.

That summer, the opportunity for me to travel abroad arose for the first time as we traveled to Germany for the 1999 Rolli Point Cup in Munich, Germany. Staying in the Olympic Village and seeing the exact spot where the Israeli hostage crisis took place in 1972 provided me with an example of the worst of what mankind is capable of—the antithesis of the values of sport. Sport, like no other element in society, helps us to bridge the gap between race, ethnicity, gender, age, and socioeconomic class. It doesn't matter what color you are, how much education you have or don't have, where you live or where you are from, sports provide an opportunity to bond and give people a common ground when they may share nothing else in common.

After winning the Cup, I won another MVP award, which further cemented my status at the time as the best 1.5 in the world, as my closest competitor from Belgium played in the same tournament. Ceruti and I got a Eurorail pass and took a twelve-hour train ride from Munich to Rome, Italy. Here I was headed to Rome eight years after I thought I was Marco Polo after my first rugby trip—a 120-mile trip from Chicago to Champaign. While a twelve-hour train ride may seem long, the scenery of the Alps and the richness of the Italian countryside made the trip go by rather quickly. In Rome, we experienced the Vatican, the Sistine Chapel, and, of course, the Roman Coliseum. Seeing so much history in a place that once was the center of the world was indescribable. And being on such hallowed ground where the Apostle Paul once walked, and where they fed Christians to lions, really allowed me to be thankful that the Lord had blessed me so richly as well as appreciate the sacrifices others made before me. I saw maps encased of the "new continent" from European explorers drawn up shortly after Christopher Columbus arrived in America. These maps were limited to what had been discovered at the time, which was the Eastern seaboard of the United States, and ended at the southern tip of Florida. I sat there in amazement at the precision of these maps which appeared as if they could've been taken off of satellite imagery but were drawn by surveyors on a boat obviously without the benefit of an aerial view. That moment I realized the greatness that human beings possess when they seek to fulfill their God-given gifts.

We climbed on the train after three days and headed back for Munich. Rudy's flight was a day before mine. So I got off the train in Florence, spending a day there after checking into the hotel I previously reserved. The birthplace of the Italian Renaissance,

Florence, is the most beautiful city I've ever seen, as I stayed a block away from the Palazzo Vecchio, the site of Michelangelo's Statue of David. To say the sport of rugby helped me to travel, see, and experience the world would be an understatement.

After the 1999–2000 season and winning the 2000 Athlete of the Year, I was ready for what would be the last epic event of my rugby career. In the spring of 2000, I tried out for and once again made Team USA, which would compete in the Sydney Paralympics in late October. While '96 Atlanta was the pinnacle of my career, '00 Sydney became the coronation. I made the decision the prior season to retire from the game after nine seasons. And even though I came back after two years off to play three more seasons on the club team level with the Generals and even coach for a season in 2005–2006, the Sydney Games were my last as a member of Team USA. By this time, I had reached all my goals, without any real challenges remaining to motivate me. Four plus years of traveling and playing year-round wore on me and, finally, I met my soul mate Amy, whom I married the following January. So although ready for rugby to be over, I cherished every moment of my Sydney experience.

Australia isn't much different from the States other than the accents and that they drive on the opposite side of the road like in the UK. Unlike Europe, Australia is modern in its construction and architecture, having come to age in the last century. The people themselves are as friendly as they come and the attention given to the Paralympics was one hundred times that of Atlanta. You couldn't go anywhere in Sydney without the guy on the train next to you or the couple sitting at the next table in the restaurant engaging you in a conversation like you were a long-lost friend. In Atlanta, the media and fan attention was more local, while in Sydney the national press (print and broadcast) covered the Paralympics and fans came from across the country. The fanfare was incredible; as in Atlanta, we were unable to go anywhere without being asked for an autograph or to pose for a picture. The difference was in the much larger volume of people attending the various events. They constructed the venues near one another so you could walk, or roll, from event to event, which were always packed near capacity. In and around the venues, we needed actual escorts by our able-bodied support staff, equipment manager, and Australian security personnel to control the wave and onslaught of intense fan attention.

Opening ceremonies again provided me with an event I completely soaked in while realizing I would never again enter a stadium amongst other athletes at the top of their game with tens of thousands of people packing a stadium to see us. Coming through that tunnel once more with the flickering cameras and the lights reflecting off of all the colors within the stadium was simply incredible. But the rugby, both on and off the court, would by far set these Paralympics apart from anything any of us ever saw before or since.

Australians really hold a deep appreciation for sport and, in particular, rugby, which is as popular over there as football is in the U.S. More so than with any other sport, the Aussies really fell in love with wheelchair rugby. We played in an actual dome constructed for our sport. I remember the walk-through (or roll-through) the night before the eight-team tournament started and how in awe we all were in just looking around at the immensity and modernity of the facility. The crowds packed every game, even early pool play games, to capacity. But the further the tournament went on, the more the lines formed outside with people waiting anxiously hours before the games for tickets. Rugby, like no other sport, including basketball, took over the attention of the Paralympics. Rugby commanded the headlines on the sports pages, helped in large part by the success of the Australian national team.

When our national team assistant coach from 1996, Reggie Richner, led Sharp Shadow to the National Title in '97 and again in '98, he was appointed to head coach. In 1999, Terry Vinyard accepted the head coaching position with Australia and looked to elevate the Aussies from sixth in the world straight to the top. I joked with Terry before the Paralympics that their nickname should be the "Silver" Platters, as they'd be doing well to finish behind us. Well, those words almost came back to haunt me. In the semifinals, we easily dispatched our old rival Canada while the fifth-seeded Aussies in an epic overtime battle upset their heated rival and second-seeded New Zealand. Of all the rugby I've ever seen as a fan, this game was the most intense not only because of the high caliber of play by both teams but also because of the sheer intensity of the sell-out and largely Australian crowd of 15,000 (5,000 more waited outside in overflow seating), setting a record to be equaled the next day for the Gold Medal game. Some of the players were so exhausted after the game that they had to be pushed into the locker rooms—the only time in wheelchair rugby I've ever witnessed this!

The next day as I headed for our bus from the Olympic Village to the arena, I passed by the Australian team. Terry just looked at me, smiled, and said in front of his guys, "Remember when you called us the Silver Platters. Well, here we are."

I thought, *Great, I just gave these guys some unintended bulletin board material.* We prepared well for the Aussies and knew their crowd would help carry them as ours did in 1996. As boisterous as expected, the "Aussie, Aussie, Aussie ... Oi, Oi, Oi" chants rang throughout the Dome before the game even started. An estimated eight million viewers watched the game on TV as the electric atmosphere crept across Australia. The game itself was close as well as intense. The Australians actually took a three-goal lead late in the third quarter. With the ball, the Aussies played keep-away before we forced a turnover and stole the momentum of the game. We took the lead midway through the fourth quarter and then withstood a valiant late-game surge to hold on 32–31.

Whereas I felt exhilaration in '96, I now felt relief just to survive in winning another Gold. Team USA went 46–0 in international competition since 1990 and 19–0 since I joined the team in 1996. Ultimately, our National teams would go ten years, from 1992 to 2002, without losing a game, an impressive run unlikely to be equaled, with the rest of world eventually catching up in the development and talent of their teams. The pressure of staying on top is overwhelming in the face of teams and players constantly raising their game to compete with you. I took my place alongside my teammates on the medal stand watching the raising of the American flag during the National Anthem. With Amy and my parents in attendance, a feeling of achievement, fulfillment, contentment, and peace filled me. I thanked the Lord once again for blessing me so tremendously by allowing me to go from someone unable to get out of a hospital bed to a rookie player who couldn't get off the bench to a World Champion to Athlete of the Year and two-time Paralympic Gold Medalist. A month later, we were off to D.C. to tour around, visit the White House, and ultimately meet President Clinton. Regardless of political affiliation and whether one likes or dislikes this president or that president, the level of holding the office with the work and effort it takes to get there is worthy of respect. And having the opportunity to shake the hand of my country's president would go down as another career milestone written forever in my memory.

With rugby behind me, I looked forward to marrying Amy, and at that point Romans 8:28, "And we know that in all things God works for the good of those who love him, who have been called according to his purpose," gave me the full meaning and purpose of the events over the previous decade. While the circumstances of my injury could have been devastating and tragic, God took those events and began to use me in fulfilling a greater purpose while allowing me to have a life greater than any I could ever imagine.

SECTION V

The Best of Times (2001–Present)

I vividly remember four events from 1999: my brother Dave got married, my brother Steve and I took a trip to the Football Hall of Fame in Canton, and my childhood hero (the great Walter Payton) passed away at forty-five from liver cancer. But the fourth event always standing out was meeting Amy Lee Woods in December 1999 at our church, Idlewild Baptist, in Tampa. The first time I saw her a month prior, I was sitting in the back row before a service, and as she walked by me, I remember thinking how sweet and beautiful she looked. At this time, a "girlfriend" was really the last thing on my mind as I geared up for and focused on training and making the Paralympic team. So I didn't think much of it when a buddy of mine, who jokingly referred to her as my girlfriend, told me she was engaged to a hockey player. Apparently, my friend walked in late to a conversation at a restaurant and heard Amy, who always joked around, telling everybody at the table about her "fiancé" and then pulling a picture out of her purse of none other than Steve Yzerman of the Detroit Red Wings. So, of all things, my future wife was a diehard fan of a team I loathed as the main rival of my team, the Chicago Blackhawks. My friend had no idea she was referring to "Stevie Y." Well, after about a week of thinking she was engaged to a minor league or junior hockey player, my buddy cleared up his misunderstanding of the situation. I thought *Great! Now I'm in business and need to try to get to know this girl.*

I started praying for an opportunity for the Lord to open up a door and thus my roommate and I planned a dinner party with a few select invitees. Obviously, the focus for me was trying to get to know Amy. Well, when I returned from a rugby tournament in Phoenix, Arizona, my roommate informed we didn't need to host a party because Amy and her friend were actually hosting a party and we both were invited. Unfortunately, the flu nailed me the day before and I couldn't make the party. As I lay on the couch, my phone rang, and once the "old fashioned" answering machine picked up, I heard a sweet voice (who to this point I had never talked to) saying she was sorry I was sick. I quickly bounced up off the couch, hit *69 to call back the number, and we spoke for the first time, probably for a total of two minutes. Now to this day, Amy says that at that point she didn't even know who I was other than "the guy in the wheelchair." Her friend asked my roommate where I was when he arrived and after explaining that I was sick, Amy responded, "Who is Bill?" Her friend said, "You know, the guy in the wheelchair," which prompted Amy to call to tell me that she sent a plate of food home with my roommate. No matter though; the door had been opened and God began to work.

Amy called again two days later when I didn't make it to church. I told her I felt better and then asked if I could call her when I got back from Houston, Texas. I'd be traveling there the following weekend for the first round of national team tryouts and when I called her upon return, I asked her to pray about whether or not she wanted to go out on a date with me. That Wednesday, a bunch of the "singles" from church went out to eat after the service and then to see Toy Story 2. I cared less about the movie then the chemistry evident between us. Even though with a large group, we connected as if set apart from the group as a whole. We spoke by phone the next day, two days before Christmas, and I told her I'd call her when I got back from my grandma's in South Florida where I'd be driving to and staying through Christmas Day. Upon driving home, I came up I-75 and then as I went over the Skyway Bridge toward St. Petersburg, I prayed in my car, and out loud for the first time in my life, asking God to give Amy to me and allow me to provide, take care of, and love her. That night (Christmas 1999) we spoke for almost four hours until the early hours of the morning and decided to start dating. Within three weeks, we were unofficially engaged, and on Valentine's Day 2000 (six weeks later), I gave her an engagement ring.

Neither Amy nor I recommend such quick engagements. But what can I say? It worked for us, and, although hard to explain, we felt God's hand on us. For my part, I've always been good with my sports background at recognizing talent and potential. I recognized that Amy was the real deal and I knew she had a heart for God and would make a great wife, and, eventually, a mother. And I can say looking back that she's completely fulfilled and lived up to her potential. She proved to be as sincere and genuine as anybody I've ever known. There's no difference between the Sunday morning Amy and the rest of the week Amy. There's no difference between the behind-closed-doors Amy and the out-in-public Amy. She's consistent and she is how she portrays herself as well as being as honest as anyone. In a society where people can be fake, my wife is a breath of fresh air. Topping everything off, the Lord decided to give her to me! A no-brainer for me, I snatched her up as quickly as I could. We decided on a wedding date of January 13, 2001, so I could focus on gearing up for Paralympics, and the year-long engagement also gave us time to learn, grow, and get to know each other.

Amy and I have been married for ten years now and we've had a glorious run—tough at times, challenging at others, but tremendous nonetheless. My wife is amazing for so many reasons, the highest among them being the background she has overcome. Our first real challenge as well as a test of our faith came on September 6, 2001, five days before 9/11, when Amy's biological mother committed suicide. Amy's mother dealt for years with psychological issues and they both endured a strained relationship with each other. Amy's life was one of neglect and abandonment, but we only have one biological mother, and the suicide devastated Amy. Six months later, Amy's dad, also with issues and a severe alcoholic, almost died from an illness brought on by alcohol abuse. He unfortunately passed away in July 2010, which was so sad in so many ways. The man died broken—financially, emotionally, mentally, and spiritually—with nothing but regrets. Wasted potential and regrets are no way to look back on your life. The legacy I hope to leave behind for my children is fulfilling my God-given promise, thus setting an example for them to do the same. Not everybody comes into this world with the potential to be a champion, a PhD, a Billy Graham, or a Michael Jordan. But the key is finding your potential and fulfilling it. If your potential is graduating high school with a C average and re-treading tires for a living, then do it with all your vitality. When I pass on and God calls me home, I want my funeral to be a celebration and for my children to know that their father did everything to the best of his ability as a Christian, husband, father, and man.

Anyhow, to say the first eighteen months of our marriage were challenging would be an understatement. My Facebook page states that "I'm easy to get along with for the most part and pretty much like everybody except whiners, complainers, excuse makers and underachievers." That statement sums me up and illustrates why I have so much love and respect in my heart for my wife. She's a champion, overcoming tremendous odds in her life that have destroyed people with less internal determination, desire, and focus.

Amy, oftentimes with me accompanying her, went through Christian counseling through our church for over a year to help her deal effectively with her emotional pain and disappointment that she suffered because of her mother's illness. They say that you either become what you experienced growing up or you run in the other direction. I once heard one of our pastors remark that he had alcoholic parents. When someone asked his brother why he became an alcoholic, his brother remarked, "Because my parents were alcoholics; what did you expect me to become?" When someone once asked our pastor why he never had a drink in his life, he remarked, "Because my parents were alcoholics; what did you expect me to become?" To her credit, Amy ran the other direction in her twenties from what she experienced in her formative years. For my part, that first year and a half grew and stretched me as

I learned to become a selfless partner to my lifelong teammate. Reflecting back, I went into marriage looking more for my fulfillment and happiness. Even though I asked God when I crossed over the Skyway Bridge on Christmas Day 1999 to allow me to take care of Amy, I didn't fully comprehend true sacrifice and giving of one's self. But to become successful from a team standpoint, and maintain that success once you get there, you have to be willing to change your mindset in giving of your own wants and needs for the betterment of your team, or in this case marriage.

Our Christian walk and commitment to a biblical lifestyle binds us together. I'm constantly amazed at how analogous marriage, in particular a Christian marriage, is to team sports and how the lessons learned on the playing field carried over into my marriage. I became a Christian in 1995, joining Idlewild Baptist Church in '97 soon after moving to Tampa, and at that point my spiritual growth really took off. I started memorizing and then meditating on scripture, which helped train as well as discipline my mind for a pure lifestyle in much the same way I had previously trained my body to excel at the highest level of my sport. As an athlete, the Bible really spoke to me as the Apostle Paul, who wrote most of the New Testament, consistently uses athletic metaphors to describe the Christian lifestyle, such as running a race with determination and discipline. Two verses in particular really spoke to me: "I have fought the good fight, I have finished the race, I have kept the faith" (2 Timothy 4:7) and "I press on toward the goal to win the prize for which God has called me heavenward in Christ Jesus" (Philippians 3:14). The latter verse is the perfect analogy for wheelchair rugby. In short, my spiritual training and growth prior to meeting Amy equipped me as a godly husband.

Once we were married, the value of teamwork and sacrificing for a common goal of a successful marriage paid off. Competing in team sports teaches you to quickly overlook a fault or mistake and move on if you want to be successful. In rugby, we used to say "next play" or "transition" after a mistake or turnover, as there's no time to bicker, complain, or point fingers on the court. Once some time elapses after the mistake, either during a timeout or conclusion of a game and calmer heads prevail, the time is then right to discuss and find a remedy for a problem. I've learned not to sweat the small stuff, and when you look at life through God's eyes, everything is small. One of my weaknesses is getting furious when someone is unable to see my point of view. I learned early in marriage to allow for differing opinions. Once after an argument with Amy, I prayed while in a state of anger and frustration. God reminded me of a previous argument where two weeks later I could not, for the life of me, remember why we fought. Today, I refuse to hold on to frustration for more than a few minutes when we don't see eye to eye. It's just not worth the time and stress. We talk about our feelings and frustrations while trying to see the other's point of view as well as our own shortcomings in resolving our conflict. Along those lines, my wife taught me that timing is everything and "it's not what you say but how you say it." Our communication has always been a strong suit and, as a result, we enjoy a very healthy marriage.

Vitally important to success in marriage is becoming each other's cheerleader. "As iron sharpens iron, so one man sharpens another" (Proverbs 27:17). No one should ever laugh or cry with your spouse more so than you do. When Amy went to counseling after her mother's passing, I went with her, and in the process I learned a lot about myself as well. During one session, Henry Bieber, who ran the counseling ministry at Idlewild Baptist, turned the tables on me and said he sensed I wasn't being "true to myself," that I had developed this rough exterior without ever really dealing with my disability and in some ways acted a bit phony. Although I scoffed at first and took offense because "we were there to help Amy not me," he was right. That night God revealed to me all the hurt and emotional pain I had carried around since my injury. I wept and told Amy things I felt and experiences that I had never shared with anyone prior to that time. My marriage and the loss experienced by my wife allowed me, at thirty-one years old, to begin to see inside of myself for the first time. We built a bond during that season of our marriage that we continue to strengthen by sharing all the joy and sorrow in life with one another.

On the athletic field, successful teams pick one another up when their teammate struggles; they don't point fingers—giving rise to the cliché "you win as a team and lose as a team." Marriage is no different when mistakes are made, which is why the biblical model of forgiveness becomes so important. Jesus commands us to constantly forgive while paying attention to and correcting our own faults. Too many spouses spend too much time analyzing and blaming their mate as opposed to reflecting on and praying about their own weaknesses and shortcomings which lead directly to marital conflict. Believe me, none of these principals is easy to implement and it's easier to talk about or dispense advice than put it into practice in your own marriage. But that's why all the values learned in becoming a championship team (selflessness, serving others, patience, endurance, perseverance, forgiveness) all apply to having a championship-level marriage. No coincidence—the whole of the Bible revolves around these values and attributes. Unfortunately, marriage receives a bad rap in our society, as the divorce rate soars above fifty percent. A championship-level marriage takes work and commitment. I believe so many marriages fail and the divorce rate has spiked in the last thirty years in large part because people have become lazy—not willing to put forth the effort. But marriage is beautiful: a wonderful bond and covenant with another human being where two truly become one. Marriage only breaks down when one or both partners put their own needs above their spouse but flourishes when both individuals sacrifice selflessly to honor their spouses and put their partner's needs above their own. "There's no I in team" and no room for selfishness on a team or in marriage.

Similar to my rugby career, I was blessed with and studied influential role models or Christian "teammates." Before marriage, the Lord brought people into my life through the singles ministry like Walter Oswald and Charlie Weaver. Both guys were older, as well as Christians for longer than I have been, and both taught me how to be consistent with my beliefs and lifestyle so I was the same person on Saturday night that I was on Sunday morning. After I was married, I met guys like Matt Lobel, Ray Lynch, and Bob Blair. I've been in a small group with Matt along with Ryan Bretsch and Joe Makinster for the last six years where we've worked on growing spiritually in becoming stronger men, better husbands, and more committed fathers. Ray and Bob are older mentors who've been through the rigors of marriage while raising kids and were able to provide a biblical road map to success for me to study. I grew close to Bob after his wife Doreen broke her back, becoming a paraplegic. The adjustment from being able-bodied to spending life in a wheelchair is difficult enough, but it's particularly difficult when you have three young children in the home as did the Blairs. But I saw Bob exude an unconditional love for his wife along with qualities like grace, patience, and perseverance that I've internalized and will take with me for the remainder of my life.

Marriage also mirrors team sports in the area of communication. Effective communication and learning the art of conflict resolution provide a vital building block in marriage. In the same way that an athlete needs to be in constant communication with his teammates on the court to understand and anticipate their next move while being aware of the opposition, we need to be in continual dialogue with our spouses. Good teammates are encouragers, as are good spouses. Learning how to resolve conflict is so vital because life, like a game, is fast-paced. You need to praise one another as well as talk about what went wrong while acknowledging each other's role in the problem area, correct it, and move on to the next play or game.

Don't get me wrong—I have not always been gifted in these areas and I'm still a work in progress. My wife and many of my ex-teammates will tell you that my hard-charging, strong personality has been difficult to deal with at times. An area that I've grown in because of my marriage is becoming a kinder, less "rough" or "rigid" person, as my wife would say. In a lot of ways, my edge, drive, determination, and chip on the shoulder mentality—all of which has helped make me successful—also can inhibit me from being graceful. To this day, I can get very argumentative when discussing any number of topics I'm passionate about if I feel I'm the one approaching the topic from a rational, common-sense point of view. But in marriage and with male/female relationships, "common sense" can be in the eye of the beholder. Amy constantly said to me, "You are not hearing what I'm saying," and my response was always, "I hear what you're saying. I just don't agree with you." But eventually I learned that I wasn't listening to her. I was trying to ram my point home and already formulating and thinking about my next comeback to her as she explained herself to me. Eventually, James 1:19 became a memory verse for me and is one I'm still trying to perfect in every area of my life. "My dear brothers, take note of this: Everyone should be quick to listen, slow to speak and slow to become angry." Show me any situation in life, be it in team sports or marriage, where this lesson wouldn't save a lot of problems for a lot of people.

Amy would often say in our first few years of marriage that she just needed me to be "nice." This dumbfounded me because she would also say I wasn't a mean person—I didn't yell, cuss, or beat her. So we definitely had some conflict until I realized what true "niceness," or grace, is—essentially, it's not what you say but how you say it. In short, I have the jerk gene. The Bible says that Jesus came as the perfect balance of "grace and truth." He was always truthful but His graceful words and kind demeanor allowed Him to get His message across in a manner that people would understand and respond to. I started thinking back to guys like Tony Granata, Pat Faherty, and Bob Blair, all true "good guys" who had a warm quality to their personalities, and then realized what Amy meant. If I were not a Christian and thus open to God's growing me through prayer and meditating on scripture, there's no way that light could ever go off in me for me to begin to become the husband that my wife needs.

I will always struggle with leaning more to the truth than grace side. But I'm aware of my struggles and Amy is a tremendous "teammate." She very rarely, if ever, hesitates to understand and overlook my shortcomings while "picking me up when I'm having a bad game." Of all the athletes written about in this book, there is no greater champion than Amy Renje. My wife is a treasure from God and makes it easy for me to be a better man, as she is the definition of the virtuous woman of Proverbs 31: "A wife of noble character who can find? She is worth far more than rubies. Her husband has full confidence in her and lacks nothing of value. She brings him good, not harm, all the days of her life. ... She gets up while it is still dark; she provides food for her family. ... She opens her arms to the poor and extends her hands to the needy. ... She is clothed with strength and dignity; she can laugh at the days to come. She speaks with wisdom, and faithful instruction is on her tongue. She watches over the affairs of her household and does not eat the bread of idleness. Her children arise and call her blessed; her husband also, and he praises her: 'Many women do noble things, but you surpass them all.'" I'm more in love with my wife today because of our collective hard work, effort, and growth than at any other point in our ten-year marriage.

Another core aspect of Christianity is serving others. Through my willingness to serve, the Lord would open a door for me in business where I'd again lean on my athletic experiences in catapulting to success in my professional career. I started serving as an eighth grade Sunday school teacher in 1999, wanting to help young teens going through all the perils of adolescence that I had gone through fifteen years earlier. While the popular culture changes—the styles, music, movies, and lingo—teenage pressures are cross-generational. Eighth grade is a crucial time in a young person's life as they get ready to enter high school where aspects of their lives, like driving, give them more freedom. Adolescence is a time when young people come to that fork in the road by starting to act and think on their own, independent of their parents. Up that point, kids have been living the lives their parents want them to live. They attend church because mom and dad take them there. They've been walking their parents' walk and by young adolescence, most are tired of doing what mom and dad tell them. Even though unable to head out on their own financially, teenagers begin to claim their independence emotionally, spiritually, and mentally.

My co-teacher for that year and the next six was a guy named Pat Nummy. Pat and I saw our roles as more in the realm of giving biblical guidance and support and relating our own real life experiences rather than pounding them with the "do's and don'ts" approach. Accountability became a constant theme we discussed. We continually talked about owning up to our actions while taking responsibility and learning from our mistakes. Our hope was that they would walk through adolescence and young adulthood with eyes wide open, aware of the pitfalls while avoiding so many of the negative consequences of bad actions that we experience during that period of life. Getting a teenager, especially males, to think beyond today and their socially ingrained "instant gratification" mindset is tough to accomplish. They're constantly bombarded with these types of messages through friends, television, movies, and popular culture as a whole. Guiding them to think about consequences is no easy task, as the pre-frontal cortex in males controlling the thinking through one's actions doesn't fully develop in a male until one's early twenties. But even though challenging, the reward years later of a former student's parent or a student themselves telling us what an impact we were on their lives made the effort all worth it.

Even though Pat is about fifteen years older than me, we became pretty good friends through our common bond of serving in the middle-school ministry. He was very supportive of my Paralympic effort in 2000 and continually told me that I needed to meet his two best friends, Dewey Mitchell and Allen Crumbley. Pat grew up with Allen and all three attended the University of Alabama in the '70s. Allen and Dewey played football and won a national title under Paul "Bear" Bryant. Dewey grew up north of Tampa and, along with gaining a national championship ring, also made the 1984 Olympic team in judo. So Pat was excited for all of us to meet, which we did at Allen's house for the Fourth of July in 2001. Pat told me that Allen wanted to watch the tape of the Gold Medal game from the Sydney Paralympics the previous October. It was through our interaction and subsequent get-togethers that Allen shared with me how team sports and role models like Bear Bryant played a vital role in his success as a businessman.

Allen and Dewey had bought a local mom and pop real estate company called Tropical Realty in the late '80s. They affiliated themselves with Prudential and built Prudential Tropical Realty into the most successful locally owned real estate company in the Bay Area, specializing in both residential and commercial, by 2001. So about a month after our initial get-together, Pat, Allen, and I got together again for lunch. As we sat there, I became intrigued and interested as Allen described his career in commercial real estate. Usually when people tell me about their line of business, boredom overcomes me. But I hung on Allen's every word, and even though I had never given thought to a career change, I began to reassess my future.

Since 1996 when I moved to Tampa, I worked as a counselor with people with disabilities. My role was not only to teach them how to become independent by illustrating how to do things like get themselves, and their chair, into a vehicle; I also helped them to find resources like funding outlets for home modifications. Frequently, I went into the schools to discuss disability prevention and awareness with students, talking to twenty-five kids in a classroom setting as well as 2,000 kids in auditoriums. While I found my career rewarding, it also provided me with the flexibility to train and travel for my primary career focus of rugby. But the pay, while adequate when I was single, proved dismal now that Amy and I were married with aspirations of her being a stay-at-home mom someday. And with my rugby career now over, a career in commercial real estate intrigued me as I envisioned new challenges to replace those in rugby. After meeting with Allen a few more times and with the full blessing of my wife, I decided to get my license and try my hand as a commercial estate agent and eventually a broker. Having no business background or formal business education meant that the task and climb to success would be daunting. Eighty percent of all agents wash out in the first year and Allen prepped me for this, even telling me that I'd get "bloodied" out there. Years later he'd tell me he was trying to talk me out of going into the business for my own good. Looking back, I had no right to succeed and every reason to fail—I was going into a career as a quadriplegic with no previous business experience where only two out of ten make it. But no matter—I was all in for the challenge. Once again the Lord's hand was on me and, once again, my sports background prepared me for the road ahead.

CHAPTER 11

1917

If any team in my lifetime had no business succeeding and every reason to fail in winning a championship, it was the 2005 White Sox. Eighty-eight years had passed since Chicago had witnessed a baseball world champion and 1959 was the last time a Chicago team made the World Series when the Sox lost to the Dodgers. For the first thirty-four years of my life, I grew accustomed to a lot of bad and mediocre baseball with an occasional winning season that ultimately ended up in disappointment. The Cubs got close in 1984 and 2003, needing just one win in a combined six games to reach the Series but fell short in the most horrific of ways. As for the Sox, their best shot after 1983 came in the early 1990s when they fielded their most talented teams collectively in a generation. Led by young stars Frank Thomas, Robin Ventura, and the best pitching staff in the American League, the Sox boasted the best record in Major League Baseball from 1990 through 1994. Unfortunately they were done in by the Toronto Blue Jays in the '93 American League Championship Series. The Blue Jays won all three games in Chicago en route to winning the series and ultimately became only the sixth franchise in major league history to win back-to-back World Series titles.

The year 1994 looked like the Sox's year. Thomas would win his second consecutive MVP award. And, for the second year in a row, the Sox pitching staff fronted by young phenoms led the American League in Earned Run Average. But a player's strike in August resulted in the cancellation of the rest of the season, breaking the hearts of baseball fans across the country and, in particular, places like Montreal and Chicago where our cities had a real shot of winning it all. Like the NFL work stoppage in 1987 which led to disharmony amongst management and players, as well as the unofficial end of the Bears' would-be dynasty, the '94 strike provided the undoing of the Sox. Sox owner Jerry Reinsdorf was viewed as a chief antagonist by the players on the part of the owners. Number one starter Jack McDowell's long-running feud with the front office ended when he was traded to the Yankees in the off season.

Players in the midst of their prime were either traded or left via free agency with little to nothing in value coming in return. Pitcher Alex Fernandez was allowed to leave via free agency after the 1996 season. The team traded Wilson Alvarez and closer Roberto Hernandez in late July of 1997 with the Sox only 3.5 games out of first place in the infamous "white flag" trade. Cornerstone Robin Ventura, among the best third basemen in the American League, signed with the Mets after the '98 season where he went on as one of the most productive third basemen in the National League for the next several years. The team that some thought would become the team of the 1990s never was allowed to fulfill that potential

The Sox flirted with success in the early 2000s, even winning a division title in 2000 before getting swept in the first round of the playoffs. But mostly, we saw mediocre and underachieving baseball, so much so that prior to the 2005 season, three of their best hitters were either traded or allowed to leave. Nobody expected much from the 2005 Sox as publications like *Sports Illustrated* predicted "a fall in the standings," picking the Sox to finish a distant third in their own division. But chemistry, especially in a sport like baseball, is an oft-overlooked quality in particular because it's so hard to quantify on paper. Old-fashioned values like selflessness, sacrifice, hard work, maximum effort in playing above your potential, mental toughness, and perseverance still go a long way on the playing field and in the arena of life. The 2005 Chicago White Sox epitomized all these qualities. Manager Ozzie Guillen, a former Sox player known more for his fire and grit than his talent, imparted his tenacity upon his players.

Shocking everybody, the Sox jumped out to a 35–17 start and five-game lead through May and eventually a nine-game lead at the All-Star break while peaking at 69–35 with a fifteen-game lead over Cleveland on August 1. All year long, the Sox won low-scoring games with timely hitting from players like leadoff hitter Scott Podsednik and Tadihito Iguchi, both of whom were brought in by GM Kenny Williams in the off season. Also making White Sox debuts that year were catcher A.J. Pierzynski and big-hitting Jermaine Dye. Dye resurrected his career in '05 after a string of injuries limited his production the previous four seasons. Dye complimented other power hitters in the Sox lineup such as corner infielders 1B Paul Konerko and 3B Joe Crede.

But the success of the Sox started and ended with their strong pitching. Starters Jon Garland and Jose Contreras enjoyed career years while Freddy Garcia and Mark Buerhle gave their usual steady performances. Rounding out the five-man rotation was Orlando "El Duque" Hernandez who, although past his prime, had previous championship experience. Middle relievers Neil Cotts and Cliff Politte were almost untouchable in having career years, as was closer Dustin Hermanson before a back injury forced him to give way to rookie Bobby Jenks late in the season. Still, they played better on the field than their talent level on paper. I can remember my brother Steve telling me all season long that they "are not that good," and he was still saying this in early August. No matter though; no team had ever blown such a large lead so late in the season in baseball history. So the only drama left was getting through the last two months of the season healthy enough going into the playoffs. Unfortunately two things happened along the way—the Sox started to run out of gas and Cleveland started to catch fire.

The starting pitching, the backbone of the team all season, started to falter outside of Contreras and the clutch hitting stopped. Cleveland climbed from fifteen games back on August first to 7.5 back on September first. In full freefall, the Sox held only a 1.5 game lead on September 24 with only a week left in the season. Seeing this kind of thing before, the media started writing the obituary for the 2005 season, and the usually pessimistic Chicago baseball fans all but gave up hope. And then, somehow, someway, the team mustered enough reserve strength to push through their late season fatigue in winning eight out of their final ten games, including a sweep at Cleveland the final weekend to hold off the surging Indians. Going into the postseason, the general pessimism accompanying either Chicago baseball team playing in October seemed to fade. The Sox had hit the wall in the final weeks and then fought hard enough to break through it; in essence, they looked Chicago baseball history straight in the face and spat in it.

The White Sox next went on one of the most dominating postseason runs of all time by sweeping the defending champion Red Sox 3 games to 0 before playing the Angels in the American League Championship Series. Spurred on by four complete games in a row by their starting pitchers, a feat not accomplished in the postseason since the 1920s, the Sox beat the Angels 4 games to 1, giving Chicago its first trip to a World Series since 1959. For me, an emotional moment came when the last out was recorded. After witnessing so many heartbreaks, near misses, and so much bad baseball, I never thought I'd see either the Cubs or Sox in the World Series. All the great memories of going to Sox games growing up, the family bonding, and my childhood heroes came back to me as well. I bought tickets for Games 6 and 7 of the World Series and booked a flight to Chicago from Tampa—no way I'd miss this moment. U.S. Cellular Field hosted Game 1 of the World Series. "The Cell" had been the home of the Sox since 1991 and was built across the street from the Old Comiskey after its demolition following the 1990 season. Down 4–3 in the eighth, the Astros put runners on second and third before middle reliever Neal Cotts struck out the next two hitters. Now with The Cell near delirium, Bobby Jenks came in with his 100 MPH to strike out a helpless Jeff Bagwell, ending the inning with the tying and go-ahead runners stranded on second and third base.

Jenks sent the Astros down in order in the ninth and the White Sox took a 1 game to 0 lead.

By 2005, I witnessed a lot of big moments in the World Series. I saw some big homeruns and memorable hits. Kirk Gibson of the Dodgers doing his Roy Hobbs imitation from "The Natural" against the A's in '88, former Cub farmhand Joe Carter going nuts after hitting his Series-ending homer for the Blue Jays against the Phillies in '93, and the surreal tenth inning of the "Bill Buckner" game in the 1986 Red Sox vs. Mets Series all come to mind. But never for a second did I think that I'd ever have those glorious memories of my own team doing something as dramatic as hitting a World Series–altering homerun. And in one game, Game 2, two moments occurred that forever provided those memories for me. The late October weather was vintage Chicago for that time of the year—gloomy, hazy with a slight mist, and more appropriate for football but picture perfect for fans more than willing to sit outside watching October baseball in Chicago. Game 2 was crucial as the next three games of the series would be in Houston where the Astros had the best home record in the National League.

For a while, the Astros appeared they would return home in a 1–1 Series tie as they took a 4–2 lead into the bottom of the seventh inning. The dreariness and mist had picked up around the park as the lifeless crowd looked on with two outs and one White Sox runner on base. From there, Tadahito Iguchi walked and the umpire next awarded Jermaine Dye first base. The ump thought Dye was hit by a pitch even though the ball hit the handle of his bat. All postseason the Sox capitalized on "lucky" breaks and, once again, preparation met opportunity (the definition of luck) when the most feared Sox hitter Paul Konerko stepped into the batter's box. With the Sox down by two runs, two outs, and the bases loaded, Konerko brought the crowd and Sox fans everywhere to a level of euphoria never reached by Chicago baseball fans of my generation. On the first pitch, he hit a no-doubt line drive into the left field seats to give the Sox a 6–4 lead. I probably woke up my entire block screaming "grand slam!" from the shot of adrenalin running through me. And just when I thought, as a Sox fan, that it couldn't get any better, it did in the bottom of the ninth after the Astros tied the game at 6 in the top of the inning.

With one out, light-hitting Scott Podsednik stepped into the box. Podsednik went the entire regular season with 507 at-bats and no homeruns. Astros closer Brad Lidge obviously knew this and he also knew that Podsednik had speed. Lidge therefore didn't want to walk him after going to two balls and one strike on the count. So Lidge threw him a fastball right down the middle that Podsednik drove into deep right field. My first thought was a double into the gap and, as the ball kept traveling, I thought it might hit the wall and end up a triple. A split second later the ball cleared the fence and the game was over. Bill Veeck's long-ago invention of an exploding scoreboard in Chicago lit up the night sky over the park. Podsednik rounded the bases with the crowd again roaring as they did with Konerko's homer. When Podsednik crossed home plate, the entire Sox team stood ready to embrace him. And here, in this moment, baseball, more so than any other sport, parallels the American Dream. A career journeyman (a no-name) like Podsednik who had spent his career going back and forth from the minor leagues and moving from team to team, can step up in a big moment and take advantage of his opportunity in hitting a game-winning homerun to end a World Series game. It's a dream every little boy has and plays out in his head and back yard.

The Sox went up 2 games to 0 and won the next two games in Houston in nail-biting fashion to give Chicago its first World Series Champion since 1917. I didn't need those tickets for Games 6 and 7 anymore; but I didn't care. Having already booked the plane tickets, Amy and I flew into Chicago anyway and landed the day of the championship parade. We spent the weekend soaking up the atmosphere around the city and having a lot of "I can't believe this really happened" conversations with family and friends, in particular my dad and brothers. Looking back in my lifetime, the 2005 White Sox were probably the least talented team from an individual standpoint to win a World Series. While their starting pitching was dominant, nobody outside of Mark Buehrle will likely be remembered in twenty years outside of Chicago. In a sport where the best players hit over .300, no one on the Sox hit over .290 that season.

For me personally, seeing the White Sox win a World Series provided another lesson of learning the art of patience and delayed gratification. I wouldn't have appreciated that team or the experience had they won in 1983 or '93. In the same way, I've come to appreciate the struggle, wait, and journey in other areas of my life such as career success and the joy that would eventually come from the blessings of three beautiful children.

CHAPTER 12

Another Steep Climb

In January of 2002, I completed the requirements for my real estate license and began my career with Prudential CRES Commercial Real Estate. Real estate is a low barrier to entry business requiring only a 120-hour licensing course followed by the passage of a relatively easy state exam. But success in the business is another matter as again, the rate of agents succeeding in the commercial realm beyond the first year is only twenty percent. The business is tough, especially on the commercial side, because your compensation is based on commissions from closing deals with no salary or hourly wage. If you're not closing, you're not eating, and while the commissions are typically much larger in commercial than residential, the number of deals is significantly lower. Plus, the start-up period takes a lot longer in the commercial world, as you have to learn a specific market, the properties, the ownerships, and the sales trends, in addition to properly analyzing the financials on a commercial investment deal and underwriting the value of the investment.

My career sputtered along for the first six months. Lacking a background or education in business or sales slowed my rise on the learning curve; yet I remained dogged in my resolve to achieve. Amy firmly supported me, saying all along she believed

I could do anything, including succeeding in real estate. And once again, God would surround me with a group of quality and experienced men that ultimately played an instrumental role in my success. For my real estate career, I drew upon my experiences from competing in, and following, team sports. Those experiences helped me reach success as an athlete as well as a man and now provided the same blueprint in my professional career. The major influence came when Allen Crumbley hired a veteran in the commercial real estate industry named Bill Bach. Bill, in the business in Tampa since the early 1980s, seemed to know everybody. From my sporting background, I'm able to recognize quality when I see it and I knew Bill was a guy that I wanted to get to know. He also lived in the same neighborhood as I did so it would be a geographically friendly arrangement. I saw he was working on quite a few projects and I offered up my services in assisting with any grunt work. Offering to work on bottom feeder-type assignments he lacked the time to service, I proposed we split the deals we worked together at 50/50. He agreed and the foundation of my knowledge base began to be take shape.

I spent a lot of time just absorbing Bill's knowledge in learning how to talk to and read people as well as how to prospect through cold calling. We drove around quite a bit in the car looking at properties as he taught me how to learn and study the marketplace. Bill allowed me to sit in on a lot of meetings where I simply sat, listened, and learned, following the premise that rookies are best seen and not heard. Success was slow in coming, but I started becoming more comfortable in the business. About seven months into my new career, I earned my first listing: a tiny office condo in Dade City, Florida, for a whopping asking price of $120,000. The next two deals I worked were a $350,000 little industrial building in Pinellas Park, Florida, and a $550,000 industrial deal that Bill brought me in to work with him. None of these deals provided big paydays, but they did boost my confidence to continue on my career path.

In early 2003, I found myself at another crossroads, however, as Bill Bach left Prudential CRES Commercial Real Estate for a competitor. Although making it through my first year, crucially going back to the 80/20 principal of those succeeding versus those failing, I floundered a bit without a true specialization. Commercial real estate investment is a very complex industry with four major specializations: retail, office, industrial, and multifamily. Each specialty presents a completely different area of the overall business with a varying knowledge base of expertise needed when analyzing the financials, the leases, and market comparables to formulate a value. Similar to sports, where upper-echelon athletes tend to specialize in one position within their preferred sport, top commercial agents have one area of specialization. Within their specialization, agents become experts by carving out a niche in defining a geographic area while getting to know every property and ownership within their territory. All in all, I knew I needed to hone in on an Area of Responsibility (AOR).

I started developing synergy with an agent named Casey Babb who came into the business right out of college after graduating with a Real Estate and Finance degree from Florida State. Casey started with Prudential two weeks after I did; and, after a year, he and I were the only ones left from the twenty-plus agents who started within six months of us. Again with a keen eye for talent and potential, I realized Casey possessed tremendous ability as well as a work ethic that I admired. In working together, we each exhibited complimentary attributes that strengthened the other. Casey came from a finance background, which I lacked, so his ability to financially underwrite and value a property in very detailed fashion based on the leases, rent roll, and profit and loss statements proved beneficial to our team. From my standpoint, I have an iron cast memory and am extremely structured as well as organized in the areas of administration. We discovered my abilities best served in transaction management or in negotiating and overseeing the contract to close phase of the process.

At that point, Allen Crumbley hired a guy named Mike Fields to run the commercial division. Mike previously brokered with Colliers Arnold, specializing in the sale of office buildings, and was one of their top agents in the late 1980s through the mid '90s. With Casey and me sputtering, Mike came along at just the right time and gave us needed direction. Any great coach knows the buttons to push in terms of what to demand of his players, as well as putting those players in positions to experience the most successful outcomes. Mike knew exactly what buttons to push with Casey and me. He's the one who helped us develop a partnership and define the roles each of us would have in contributing to the team. So we formally set up a team partnership playing to both of our strengths. Basically, both of us were responsible for lead generation through prospecting, attending business development meetings with prospective clients, and listing presentations. Casey's main responsibility was formulating a value range of the property as well as preparing the marketing information. He acted as the primary point of contact during the marketing phase. Once one of our properties went under contract, I became the primary point of contact until closing, as I possess a unique ability to stay focused on the big picture of closing deals. I managed the contract and oversaw the property inspections, facilitated contact between buyer and seller, and handled the negotiations on any problems as well as the subsequent remedies while under contract. In any real estate transaction, a multitude of parties are involved, often with competing or differing interests: from the buyer to the seller, lender to the appraiser, buyer's attorney to the seller's attorney, property inspector, and the title agent. My job kept everyone focused on moving forward within our contract parameters, with the big picture of getting the deal done.

In essence, Casey started and I closed in functioning as a team. The advantage in a team set-up such as ours was allowing me to prospect for new opportunities simultaneous to Casey performing his main function of promoting our current inventory of available listings. Likewise, our set-up allowed Casey to forget about a listing once it went under contract, freeing him to prospect for new business. Mike guided us in setting up a business plan and, most importantly, picking a specialization—which became the sale of apartment buildings between ten and two hundred units in the Bay Area. He helped us set goals for prospecting, winning listings, and ultimately deciding the dollar volume we wanted to achieve. Through our monthly accountability meetings with Mike, we grew steadily for the rest of 2003 before hitting our stride while fulfilling our potential starting in 2004 and peaking in 2006. Mike pounded home the importance of consistent prospecting. A very repetitious person, Mike brought a bag lunch and ate the same kind of sandwich every day. My personality, going back to my upbringing and what I saw with my father, was very similar. So I bought into Mike's system and replicated his patterned behavior. Plus, Mike had a proven track record of success, making it easy to follow his lead. From there, I committed to a daily regimen of cold calls while constantly trying to elevate and perfect my craft.

The main focus of our cold calls was providing good, quality information to owners by informing them of sales comparables and rental trends in the surrounding area to their properties. Over the course of time and consistent calling, the rapport built up with that owner ideally leads to a face-to-face meeting. Once a name is associated with a face, the hope is to develop a relationship with the property owner so someday he'll hire us to list and sell his property. For his part as our "job coach," Mike never accepted excuses. In his words, if owners weren't responsive or didn't return our voicemails, then the reason lay with something we said or how we said it. To the excuse of people not calling us back, Mike often commented that some inflection in our voice must have indicated a lack of expertise or confidence. Like with my rugby coach, I'd disdain Mike at times, but that resulted from his pushing us to excel. In the end, I appreciated him for getting the best out of me.

Not the first or the last time, I saw the definition of luck positioned front and center in my life. We prepared diligently for the first two years of our careers and opportunity presented itself to us as the market rose then peaked while we started coming into our own as quality agents. Casey and I sold our first apartment building, a thirty-six-unit deal for $1.4 million in August of 2003 and, consequently, we started to develop a track record and résumé in the apartment market. Over the next three years, through the end of 2006, we put ourselves in the right position and capitalized on the best real estate market in a lifetime. Ultimately, we closed forty-four deals, totaling $140 million and 2,590 apartment units. Our team won the Top GCI (Gross Commission Income) for the Prudential CRES Tampa office annually from 2003–2006 as we were awarded the prestigious Chairman's Circle Award Winner in 2004, 2005, and 2006, representing the top six percent of sales associates within the Prudential CRES national franchise network.

Ego can be a detriment to any team or partnership and is something to always channel properly. Realistically, great performers in any walk of life, certainly sports or business, possess big egos which drive them to excel at their profession. Again though, the key is finding the balance between confidence and arrogance by understanding that the success you've been blessed with is only possible through the combined efforts of those around you. Neither did Casey or I take credit when times proved good nor point fingers when we experienced the market crash after 2006. When times are tough, playing the blame game and pointing fingers can ruin chemistry in teams, businesses, and families.

Although we butted heads on occasion, Casey and I never let egos get in the way of where we were going. We went through all the growing pains early on that teammates and partners go through—experiences that either make or break you. With two headstrong, driven people, conflict was inevitable. We clashed over a multitude of issues, from the look and content of our team newsletter to each other's style of negotiating. But winning was the main goal, and we learned to adapt as well as overlook certain things that individually we would do differently while appreciating how our styles complemented each other. I brought maturity and a conversational approach with our clients while Casey brought youth and enthusiasm. Both sets of attributes were invaluable in opening up the doors to different sets of clients. Regardless of age, we both bonded well with those that fit our personality types, and over time we were able to discern who would be a better point of contact for each individual client.

For me individually, my professional peak came in October 2006, when I achieved the PhD of the commercial real estate industry by receiving my Certified Commercial Investment Member (CCIM) designation. Only six percent of the estimated 150,000 commercial real estate practitioners nationwide hold the CCIM designation, which reflects not only the caliber of the program but also why CCIM is one of the most coveted and respected designations in the industry. Two years prior, I began the CCIM curriculum, which consists of four core courses. Each course concludes with the end-of-course exam incorporating the essential skill sets: financial analysis, market analysis, user decision analysis, and finally investment analysis for commercial investment real estate. Ultimately by the fall of 2006, I completed the four courses and passed the minimum threshold of $30 million in sales volume needed for the designation. So I submitted my portfolio of qualifying experience then took and passed the comprehensive final exam. As much fulfillment as I received from my professional and athletic accomplishments, the rewards and joy in my personal life would soon surpass anything I could ever achieve from my external résumé.

CHAPTER 13

Team Renje

By the summer of 2006, Amy and I had been married for five and a half years but had yet to experience the joy of parenthood. Unable to conceive, we began to seek the help of a fertility doctor in early 2005, an endeavor that proved fruitless. My outlook for parenthood was pretty laidback and I trusted God's timing. Amy's goal, on the other hand, was to be a mother by the time she was thirty. So she started to feel the pressure as she turned twenty-eight in February of 2005. Amy was born for motherhood. From the time we met, she never really expressed any career desires other than becoming a fulltime mother. She loved kids and received her fix early in our marriage as she nannied fulltime for her best friend's newborn twins. But after four years into our marriage, no kids began to wear on Amy emotionally. That said, we stayed steadfast in our belief and hope and clung to the promise of God's Word in Matthew 6:33, "But seek first his kingdom and his righteousness, and all these things will be given to you as well."

On a stormy night in June of 2005, we attended a presentation at our church by an adoption ministry called Bethany Christian Services. Long in favor of adopting, I once told my friend Dave Ford that I'd love to adopt someday and give a child a shot at a quality life that otherwise would have no opportunity. Amy was definitely in favor of adopting but wanted to have a child first. That all changed after the Bethany presentation when both of us left with the overwhelming desire for adoption. The question then became where we should adopt from—the domestic route or foreign adoption, and if we pursued an international adoption, which country would be best. We started to pray and over the course of a couple of weeks still had no answer. Amy, in particular, started to get anxious and lose sleep. One night as she lay there at three in the morning, she said "God, you just need to show me where we need to go."The next morning while working her job as an office manager in a doctor's office, a patient called in to get a prescription for an antibiotic. The patient explained that she was traveling out of the country and wanted the antibiotic with her as a precautionary measure. When Amy asked where she was going, the women said she and her husband were traveling to Guatemala to pick up a baby boy they were adopting. And with that, Amy received her answer to prayer. She called me and said we were going to Guatemala. I was excited as God quickly worked at preparing my heart. Amy had a Columbian coworker whose five-year-old boy was simply adorable, and I remember thinking beforehand how I would be partial to a Hispanic boy.

We next submitted our paperwork to Florida Home Studies and Adoptions, a Christian-based agency specializing in Guatemalan adoptions. To say we filled out "paperwork" is a bit of an understatement. If our government would require anywhere near the mountain of paperwork for incoming immigrants and/ or visitors, the problem of illegal immigration and terrorist threats would dissipate quickly. The various checks included original birth certificates, work/education history, character references, criminal checks, credit checks, and fingerprints, all of which had to be notarized and approved by the U.S. Embassy and the Guatemalan government. To request, fill out, and submit the portfolio of documentation took us three months.

Amy settled on the name of Nicolas (Nico) John Renje, as my middle name is John, before switching the middle name to Allen to reflect her brother's middle name. On a Saturday afternoon, we met with the woman and her husband who had unknowingly given Amy the inspiration to go to Guatemala. We wanted to pick their brains to better understand the process and potential pitfalls. Also, for the first time we met their beautiful little baby boy who enlarged our hearts all the more for our future little boy. When we asked his name upon arriving at their house, his mother said, "Nicolas John, but we call him Nico," which simultaneously gave both Amy and me chills while further confirming God's plan for us to adopt. In November, all of our paperwork was finally submitted and we received our first baby referral which gives you the option to accept or move on to the next referral. We immediately fell in love with the newborn photos of Jorge Mario Rodriguez-Lasiter born on November 7, (my brother Dave's birthday) 2005. Now the waiting began as our adoption advocate told us the final approval process through Guatemala would take three or four months. We thus assumed Nico would be home with us in March or April of 2006.

So we began our wait as Amy left her job in January "to nest" and get ready to finally be a mother. We received email pictures of Nico as our love for him continued to grow in our hearts. He was well-provided for in a foster home with a loving family, which obviously gave us comfort during our wait. We were blessed with talented friends who painted a Noah's Ark mural on the four walls in Nico's future room. And then March came and went with April turning into May and May turning into June. Every Friday I called our advocate and every Friday she told me to call her the following week. Eventually we found out that through corruption within the Guatemalan adoption agencies the Guatemalan government threatened to close the doors to international adoptions. This action would stop on-going adoptions in process. This news devastated us, especially Amy, who by June expected to be a mother. She had stopped working five months prior and was anxiety-ridden as her days consisted of waiting for the phone to ring and checking emails.

Although everyone meant well, we couldn't go anywhere without someone asking us "when are you going to get your son?" We couldn't get around the block while walking the dog or even from the parking lot into church without someone asking us, all of which wore on Amy as her lifelong ambition of being a mother seemed just out of reach. In July, we received another blow when, six months after we submitted our paperwork, we were booted from the final stage of approval because my name affidavit was wrong. Basically, we submitted a signed and notarized list of every variation of our names (like I said, the paperwork process was cumbersome). My formal name is William John Renje Jr. and a lot of variations exist within my name: i.e., Bill Renje, Bill Renje Jr., Billy Renje, William Renje, William John Renje, Will Renje, etc.

Well, somewhere along the line, someone within the Guatemalan bureaucracy saw that one of my "aliases" didn't match up with a name used on another form I filled out. So now we had to fill out the form again and go back through the cycle of having it notarized, sending it off for approval by the state of Florida, and then mailing it to the Guatemalan embassy with no guarantees our place in line would be kept for us.

With no further clarity by mid August, Amy and I started to hit the wall, and every bit of knowledge that I could muster from my sporting background began to payoff. Amy had enough and through tears told me that if the adoption didn't go through that I needed to have someone come in and paint over the mural in the bedroom and take everything out, as the room was already prepared for Nico's arrival. As her "teammate," I tried lifting her up through prayer and kept thinking as well as talking about "running the race" with endurance and perseverance. The verse that kept coming to mind was "Be strong and take heart and wait for the Lord" (Psalm 27:14). But ultimately, our collective "teammates," our closest friends and family members, rallied around us. Specifically, our Bible fellowship class picked us up and provided energy and emotion for us through prayer. Amy literally said she had run out of gas and couldn't even pray anymore. Our class prayed fervently and, for the first time in my life, I truly felt myself uplifted and filled spiritually through the prayers of others.

I now fully knew what Paul was referring to when he talked about the body of Christ in 1 Corinthians 12:

The body is a unit, though it is made up of many parts; and though all its parts are many, they form one body. So it is with

Christ. ... Now the body is not made up of one part but of many. If the foot should say, "Because I am not a hand, I do not belong to the body," it would not for that reason cease to be part of the body. And if the ear should say, "Because I am not an eye, I do not belong to the body," it would not for that reason cease to be part of the body. If the whole body were an eye, where would the sense of hearing be? If the whole body were an ear, where would the sense of smell be? But in fact God has arranged the parts in the body, every one of them, just as he wanted them to be. If they were all one part, where would the body be? As it is, there are many parts, but one body.

The eye cannot say to the hand, "I don't need you!" And the head cannot say to the feet, "I don't need you!" On the contrary, those parts of the body that seem to be weaker are indispensable, and the parts that we think are less honorable we treat with special honor...so that there should be no division in the body, but that its parts should have equal concern for each other. If one part suffers, every part suffers with it; if one part is honored, every part rejoices with it.

And there you have it, a true functioning team at its core, one that goes through adversity and trials ultimately on its way to winning a championship and that exudes and embodies a biblical foundation.

By mid September we still persevered and were given clearance to travel to Guatemala to pick up our little boy. We had hoped Nico could celebrate his first birthday on November 7 with us, and now we'd see our desire come to fruition. On my dad's birthday on September 25, Amy and I flew from Tampa to Miami and on to Guatemala City. Guatemala, from an aerial view, is simply gorgeous with its beaches and backdrop full of rolling hills with plush trees and mountains. And once you get out of the city, the scenery is very pleasant and comparable to the Western part of the United States but much more historic with their ancient Mayan ruins. But the city reflects an impoverished country with its pollution and crowding—pollution so thick, you can taste the blackness from the poor air quality. One aspect of Guatemala I grew to admire during the short period of time we were there was the work ethic of the people. Although they had few possessions, they were willing to sacrifice and work hard. You didn't see beggars or pan handlers the way you would in U.S. cities, and at 5:00 a.m. the city is already in motion with people crowding the streets and buses on their way to work or school.

Upon our arrival, the plan was to check in at the hotel around two and then wait in the room until we received a call that the foster mom, attorney, and translator had arrived in the lobby. Well, as we checked in, before preparing ourselves for the anticipation to come, we heard a feminine Hispanic accent behind us say "Renje." As we turned, there stood a very nice woman named Sheny Hidalgo, along with her teenage daughter Paola, holding our eleven-month-old chunky little boy. She pointed at him and said "Nico," and by this time I held the camcorder as she handed off Nico to Amy. Nico put his right hand on Amy's shoulder and with the left began to reach and look back at Sheny, who he'd been with almost from birth, before stopping halfway and finally embracing Amy as if he just knew she was his "mama." After a few minutes, Amy took the camcorder and handed Nico off to me, and for the first time in my life a child unfamiliar with me didn't cry when I took hold of him. We proceeded to sit down in the lobby with our son, Sheny, and Paolo. With their English about as good as our Spanish, we tried our best to make small talk which more or less resulted in pleasant smiles and pointing at Nico. Finally, the attorney and translator arrived and, sadly, Sheny and Paola left as we promised through the translator that we'd keep up with photos and emails, which we try to do to this day.

We signed off on the pertinent documentation and set up an appointment the next day with the U.S. Embassy for the final task before departing back to the United States. Amy and I were both struck by the amount of people that lined up outside the Embassy. When asked, our translator explained that they came everyday hoping to be one of the handful able to get a visa to come to the U.S. Unfortunately for most, the dream never materialized.

The only excitement left was the plane ride home as we expected a few friends at the airport to greet us. I sat amazed on the flight home, although not surprised, at how well my wife naturally fit her role as a mother those first few days with feeding, bathing, and caring for Nico. And my amazement grew as he adapted so well as if he were waiting for us as long as we were waiting for him. A few minutes after takeoff, Nico threw up all over his American flag shirt with a businessman cowering next to us as he attempted to avoid the vomit. Undaunted, Amy cleaned Nico up like she had done it a thousand times.

Upon finally exiting the plane in Tampa, we wearily hopped on the monorail and were overwhelmed upon exiting to a standing ovation. A few dozen or so from our adoption group and Bible fellowship class awaited, complete with cameras flashing and signs, to greet us and meet Nico. Arriving home with 100 Super Bowl trophies or Stanley Cups couldn't have given me a better feeling. The celebration and parade of people from neighbors, family, and coworkers continued over the next few days. Our son was home and our dream complete. I reflected on my most recent life journey over the previous couple of years as we sought to build a family. During those precious early days with our new son, Amy and I realized that we couldn't get pregnant because God had planned all along for Nico to be our son. In the same way that Christians are biblically adopted into God's family and grafted into His heart through Jesus, Nico was grafted into our hearts. One of our most cherished poems is framed and displayed in our home and says:

Not Flesh of My Flesh
Not flesh of my flesh
Nor bone of my bone
But miraculously my own.
Never forget, even for a minute,
You weren't born under my heart,
But in it.
—Author Unknown

We enjoyed our first year with our Nico and began, or I should say Amy began, talking about a little brother or sister for Nico to round out our family. Most couples fear they won't love their adopted child as much as their biological children. Our big fear, however, was the opposite. We feared not being able to love our biological children as much as Nico. We needed to go through artificial insemination and assumed, if successful, the process would take a year or so of treatments before conception, putting Nico and the newborn four years apart, close enough to play and relate to one another. After Nico turned two in 2007, we decided to try getting pregnant. We experienced a rough go in early 2005 with the fertility treatments, an experience emotionally and physically draining on Amy. So we chose a different clinic as both of us hoped for the best but prepared for the worst. For my role, I tried to prep Amy by managing her expectations, although now, as a mother, any negative results would lack the same devastation as before.

In late December, Amy underwent her first treatment and by mid January she became convinced she was pregnant. She took seven pregnancy tests, testing positive every time. I remained in complete denial but soon changed when a blood test confirmed for us that Amy was indeed pregnant. At this point, however, elation gave way to fear when her hormone count elevated extremely high, signaling either there something wrong with the baby or there were multiples. The most fear I've ever experienced in my life came during that initial ultrasound as thoughts of reality TV shows of couples with sextuplets ran through our heads. How would we, with me already somewhat limited in a wheelchair, handle either a special needs baby or multiples? Not so coincidentally, Amy experienced twins as a nanny for her best friend's boys during the first two years of their lives. So we knew we could handle twins but certainly no more than two! As the doctor began the ultrasound, I prayed silently to God, "Lord, your

Word tells us that you won't give us more than we can handle and we *cannot* handle more than two."

With that, the doctor said, "There's one," soon followed by, "There's another one."

I replied, "So we're having twins."

"I'm not done looking," said the doctor.

Oh you better be done! I thought. My fear soon subsided with the doctor confirming only two babies. Not yet knowing the genders, Amy and I were convinced they were boys. She grew up with two brothers and I grew up with two brothers. The twins she previously took care of were boys. But the Lord pricked our heart a few weeks later when the ultrasound nurse told us that one of the babies was a girl. A very warm sensation filled our hearts with joy as Amy began to cry knowing that we'd have a baby girl. The pregnancy was rough on Amy as her morning sickness was all day sickness, but we endured until a routine visit in early July.

With a due date of October 1, a sonogram at twenty-seven weeks showed her cervix thinned to the level that she needed to go on immediate bed rest or risk premature labor. I could not take care of Nico, only two, maintain the household, and work fulltime. While blessed with a large support network, our friends all had their own stresses, struggles and commitments that come with having families and kids. We were concerned initially, but relief came to us when my mom offered to fly in from Chicago and stay with us through the remainder of the pregnancy. Helping to stabilize our household, my mom also took pressure off of Amy, who held off giving birth until September 1 when Noah David Steven (middle names after my brothers) entered the world at 4 lbs. 15 oz. followed a minute later by Daniela Renea (Dani Rae Rae as Nico would come to call her) at 4 lbs. 2 oz. Although tiny and a month early, both were healthy and allowed to come home with Amy three days later. Looking back, I'm not sure if our babies would have made it into this world without the sacrifice from my mother. These beautiful babies and the subsequent joy and fullness they've brought to our family provided yet one more miracle and example of the hand of God in our lives. Looking back, I don't think I ever truly believed I'd be a father, and now I have three kids.

Team Renje, our self-titled family name, was now complete. Another verse I memorized long before our children arrived, Proverbs 24:3–4, came to life for us: "By wisdom a house is built, and through understanding it is established; through knowledge its rooms are filled with rare and beautiful treasures." Amy and I did our best to build our family through wisdom and now God had filled our house with three rare and beautiful treasures. Our children give us so much joy as well as fulfillment and—no need for alarm—they've grown in our hearts with the same caliber of love as Nico. Nico is such a good big brother and role model. Although not obviously connected biologically, it's amazing to see the similarities of how Noah now acts as Nico did at the same age. Nico loved Disney's *Cars* and *Thomas the Train*, bringing either Thomas, Lightning McQueen, or both to the dinner table with him at eighteen months. Noah ironically now does the same thing even though he was not yet born when Nico carried out the same habits. Our little princess Dani Rae is as dainty and as precious as they come. She's daddy's little angel, as I've never seen anything so precious in all my life.

For me ultimately, I may no longer participate in organized sport, but I'm a part of the best team of my life—a team for which I'm the general manager, the head coach, and a huge fan. I relish and continue to look forward to my role in facilitating and overseeing their growth and development, knowing when to challenge and push yet also when to shower them with praise and adoration. I'm excited about managing their respective personalities while helping them find their gifts, talents, and abilities and putting them in positions to succeed based on those attributes.

I'm amazed when I sit back and realize how much I incorporate the life lessons learned from my background into my parenting and the wealth of experiences gleaned from my grandparents, parents, role models, business mentors, coaches, and teammates. In particular, I'm struck by how much I've harkened back to my own upbringing, and the parenting I received just further emphasizes the need for strong homes and parents. My mom and dad were the epitome of sacrifice, giving, and struggle. Growing up middle-class, we weren't rich, but neither did we lack what we needed. My parents often went without so we'd be able to camp as Boy Scouts, join baseball, or buy a band instrument. As a man, I often find myself dealing with my household in much the same way my dad did in his calm, collective manner. I try to be selfless as he was when it comes to my wants and needs. At one point when we were older and had jobs, my brothers and I started buying my dad clothes for Christmas, Father's Day, and his birthday. My dad never bought himself anything or asked for anything. He never once put himself above his family or said "I deserve this so I'm doing it." He could still be seen mowing the lawn wearing his faded and shrunken 1983 "Winning Ugly" AL Central Division Champion shirt in the mid '90s. I try exuding the same level-headedness as my dad who seldom ever became rattled. Although not athletic in a physical sense, my dad provided every bit the calm of a great point guard or quarterback in pressure situations within our family. My dad's brother, my Uncle Bob, once said of my grandfather, "When I was sixteen, I couldn't believe how dumb he was, and by the time I was twenty-five, I couldn't believe how much he had learned." I've used that logic in describing my dad multiple times who, through his example, has been the ultimate head coach throughout my life.

All in all, I would not have believed someone if they had shown up at my bedside within weeks of my injury to tell me what a glorious path my life would take over the next twenty years. I've also come to see from a spiritual, emotional, and mental standpoint that I can do exceeding and abundantly more than I ever would have accomplished as an able-bodied person. The Lord became my ultimate coach in first breaking me down and then building me back up. He used rugby to bring me to Florida where I met my wife, Amy. We were unable to conceive a child and now we have Nico—who may have ended up a street child in Guatemala, had the events of twenty-one years ago not taken place. We eventually conceived and now have our twins—who would not be here had the events of twenty-one years ago not happened.

The point is that we have to make the most of our tragedies, triumphs, talent, and potential. Recently, I found some of my old newspaper clippings and was struck by a quote of mine from nine months after my injury: "I'm still going to live a productive life. But

I will always be bitter and angry." Thank God the bitterness and anger has gone away and been replaced by peace and fulfillment.

My story is one of family, role models, and peers who supported and stood by my side and guided me, as well as one of a God who never gave up on me. It's one of being blessed early on with a solid foundation yet taking for granted and losing touch with that foundation. It's one of despair giving way to hope, emptiness to fulfillment, struggle to endurance, and perseverance to success. Ultimately, my life story is one of reaping the fruits of an abundant life beyond belief brought by renewal, rebirth, and resurgence.

CHAPTER 14

Remembering the Roar

The Blackhawks were the one Chicago team I stopped following after moving to Florida in 1996. Other than briefly jumping on the Tampa Bay Lightning bandwagon during their Stanley Cup run in 2004, I stopped following hockey completely, telling people back home that it was difficult to follow a winter sport when you live somewhere where the temperature is seventy degrees in January. But largely, I lost my connection to the Blackhawks because the Blackhawks lost their connection to the fans. The organization began taking for granted the foundation of love and support given to them by their loyal fan base during a lost decade of dormancy and irrelevance.

I first fell in love with the Blackhawks in 1983 for five reasons: The Indian Emblem, Pat Foley, the goal horn, Denis Savard, and the roar of the old Chicago Stadium. When I was a young child, my bedding was decorated with NHL logos with none better than the Blackhawks, whose jersey is largely considered the best in professional sports. The logo aside, you had to try hard to be a Blackhawk fan back then as they lagged well behind the city's four other professional teams in marketing and promotions. In a policy not reversed until owner Bill Wirtz died before the 2007 season, home games were not televised because Wirtz thought it unfair to paying customers to broadcast the games for free on TV. But the Blackhawks of my formative years enjoyed a solid foundation of fan support and appreciation amongst the Chicago sports crowd.

Without televised home games, my earliest Hawk memories were sitting in my room listening to the captivating voice of Pat Foley. Foley is simply the best Chicago announcer and the best announcer—period—I've ever heard. He mesmerized fans by bringing the play by play to life over the radio and into your room. I'd hang on every word as his voice would rise incrementally in describing a goal: "Savard shoots, *he scores!*" or in describing a big save by the Hawks goalie from that era, Murray Bannerman: "Here it comes, *Bannerman!*" And finally, nothing came close to the roar of the old Chicago Stadium and how much excitement you'd feel when the fog horn went off. Long before every other team sounded a siren or horn after a goal, as with the spotlight intro for the Bulls, the Stadium set the trend that was duplicated by every other arena over the following decade. I was in sixth grade in 1983, and my classmates and I talked about how cool the goal horn sounded.

But in '83, I fell in love with the Blackhawks mainly because they were winning on the ice led by a young, dynamic offensive force named Denis Savard. The Hawks enjoyed their best season in a decade in '83 led by Savard, who was third in the NHL in scoring. And although they'd get swept in the conference finals by the emerging team of the 1980s, Wayne Gretzky's Edmonton Oilers, my genesis as a Blackhawk fan had arrived. Two years later another Blackhawk tradition was born when they again found themselves in the conference finals against Edmonton. The Oilers were the defending Stanley Cup champion, in the midst of winning five

Cups in seven years, when they came to Chicago with a 2 game to
0 lead in the conference finals. To get the team going, the crowd
spontaneously started cheering during Wayne Messmer's singing of
the National Anthem. So loud was the stadium crowd, the referees
looked up at Messmer in the organ loft for a signal when he
finished. The Hawks were fired up, winning 5–2 and then tying the
series at 2 games a piece with a wild 8–6 victory two nights later.
Edmonton won the final two games of the series to advance to
the Stanley Cup finals where they again won the Cup. In addition
to increasing the Hawks' victories and adding to the mystique of
the Stadium, the series was legendary because Hawks fans haven't
stopped cheering during the anthem in the last twenty-five years.

The team sputtered over the next three seasons, but a
renaissance for Chicago hockey took place in 1989 when a new
hard-line, no nonsense coach named Mike Keenan took over.
Keenan, along with a nineteen-year-old center named Jeremy
Roenick, lifted the Hawks amongst the elite teams in the NHL
where they remained through 1996. The early '90s were glorious
times for both co-inhabitants of the Stadium. Both the Hawks
and Bulls played in their sport's conference finals in 1989, 1990,
and 1992 with both advancing to their respective championship
series in '92. Spring in Chicago is always the greatest time of the
year. Winter is behind you, summer is in front, and when both the
Hawks and Bulls are winning, there's a playoff game every night.

On a gorgeous April night in 1989, I went to my first Blackhawk
game. When I was growing up, my dad was big on taking us to
baseball games but not so much basketball, football, or hockey. So
it was not until high school when, along with three of my buddies,

I went to the Chicago Stadium for the first time—Game 5 of the Norris Division Finals (conference semifinals) against St. Louis. I've been to stadiums and arenas all over the country, including historic parks like Fenway Park, Yankee Stadium, Boston Garden, Comiskey Park, Wrigley Field, and Soldier Field, as well as modern arenas like the United Center where the Hawks and Bulls play now. I sat in the St. Pete Times Forum in Tampa when the Tampa Bay Lightning won Game 7 of the 2004 Stanley Cup Finals. Yet, I've never experienced the electricity or energy anywhere else they way I did in the Chicago Stadium. From the roaring of the National Anthem, cheering through every hard hit and every big save that night by Blackhawk goalie Alain Chevrier, and the bellowing of the goal horn after all three Hawk goals, the stadium was crazed. Also the first of its kind, the size and decibel level of the organ pulsated throughout the stadium while energizing the crowd.

No greater drama exists in sports than a one-goal playoff game, and with the Hawks winning 3–2, taking a 3–1 series lead, the party spilled over into the parking lot with delirious fans. The Hawks lost the next round against Calgary in the conference finals, but we knew we had a team on the rise, and the 1990s would be our era.

Unfortunately, though, the Hawks always came up short among the elite of the NHL. They lost again in the 1990 conference finals to their old nemesis, the Edmonton Oilers, who went on to win the last of their five Cups. In 1992, they finally beat Edmonton in the conference finals by sweeping them 4 games to 0. And with the Bulls in the NBA Finals that year, it looked like the Chicago Stadium would become the first arena ever with both basketball and hockey teams winning championships in the same year. While the Bulls held up their end, the Hawks were swept by the Pittsburgh Penguins. The games were close with the Penguins winning the four games by a total of just five goals, but Pittsburgh was more talented, having won for the second year in a row. The indwelling memory of Jeremy Roenick, the Hawks star center, would be a young fan crying as Roenick skated off with the Penguins hoisting the Cup on the Stadium ice after the Game 4 loss.

My injury took place that summer of '89 after my first trip to the Chicago Stadium. More than anything else, going to the Stadium and then to the United Center, when it opened in 1994, for Bulls and Blackhawk games provided great bonding experiences with my brothers, Dave and Steve. Once again, my hobby and passion for Chicago sports played a role in my healing, this time with the relationship with my brothers. I bought up as many standing-room-only tickets as I could for Bulls and Hawks playoff games back then, taking close friends like Tony Granata as well as my brothers.

I am the oldest, Dave is three years younger than I am, and Steve is seven years younger. So I poured every ounce of sports knowledge I had into them growing up, in particular teaching both baseball and Steve football. I often quizzed them on team logos. We have an old family video of Steve at five years old acting like a sports announcer while rattling off team names like the "Wams (Rams)" as if he were Brent Musberger on the NFL Today.

When he was six, I taught him how to be a running back by illustrating the holes he would need to run through. I'd do this by lining up plastic decorative ducks we had around our bushes in front of our house. On the right side was the 2 hole (between center and guard), 4 hole (guard and tackle), 6 hole (outside of tackle), and the same on the left side with the 1, 3, and 5 holes. As the quarterback, I called the play (32 dive) and drilled him over and over again until he got it right. During any family gathering, my dad or uncles would always have a game on television, so sports constantly provided a bonding experience within my family.

But like with everything else, I lost direction in my adolescent years. And, even though we lived under the same roof, my brothers and I lost our connection. My youngest brother Steve, years later, said I just wasn't around back then. I stopped going to his games, didn't go on family outings or even vacations, using work or summer school as an excuse. So watching as well as attending games again helped us to reclaim the bond from our youth. To this day, I call as well as text my dad and brothers back and forth during big games as geography now separates us from watching together in person. So looking back, I cherish those memories.

In 1994, the Chicago Stadium gave way to the new United Center built across the street. The UC was completely wheelchair-accessible whereas the stadium lacked elevators. So now when I bought standing-room tickets, I took the elevator up to the nose-bleed seats like everybody else. Don't get me wrong, I love the

UC and all its amenities, but I miss the charm as well as the history of the old Stadium. That last season of 1993–94, the marketing slogan for the Hawks was "Blackhawk hockey. Remember the Roar" (the goal horn sound).

After the loss in the '92 Cup Finals, the Blackhawks would make two more serious runs in that era (before ownership poisoned the team). But they lost in the 1995 conference finals to the rival Red Wings who were at the beginning of their dynasty and then in '96 to the Colorado Avalanche. I was there in attendance for Games 3 and 4 in the '95 series as well as Games 4 and 6 of the '96 conference semifinals when they were eliminated in OT by Colorado, marking the era's official end.

Frustration started to set in 1996. It looked like the Hawks' run was coming to an end before they'd be able to hoist the Cup— and not because of what was happening on the ice. With another great season, the Hawks finished third in the conference behind Colorado and Detroit before losing to Colorado in the conference semifinals 4 games to 2. The series was close as the Renje crew once again sat in attendance when, with a 2–1 series lead, the Hawks lost Game 4 in double overtime. When they lost Game 5 in Colorado, I left my brothers at home and took a date with me for Game 6 with the Hawks needing to win to force a Game 7. Rumors had been circling for a while about the future of twenty-six-year-old star Jeremy Roenick. Hawks owner Bill Wirtz had a long-standing reputation about fighting with star players, usually over money, earning him the nickname "Dollar Bill." Roenick, along with goalie Ed Belfour and defenseman Chris Chelios, was a pillar for the team. So with Roenick due for a big contract, the natural thing to do for a team always in contention with Roenick as their best player would be to pay the man. But that wasn't the Wirtz way. There was precedent when the greatest Hawk player of all time, Bobby Hull, fought with Wirtz and eventually left the Hawks for a bigger payday in Winnipeg in 1973.

Still, there was no way I thought they'd trade Jeremy Roenick. So as I looked down on the ice from my seat after the Hawks season ended in overtime, I thought I'd again see him in a Hawk jersey even as he waved and bowed to a cheering crowd, acknowledging this may be his last moment with the Indian crest on his jersey. In Atlanta a couple of months later while getting ready for the Paralympics, one of our support staff members told me the Hawks had traded Jeremy Roenick. *No way,* I thought, suspecting it was a joke; but it wasn't. Even more so than Denis Savard, Roenick resonated with me as the greatest Hawk of my lifetime and now he was gone—and so was that glorious Blackhawk era from 1989–96. The next year, Dollar Bill shocked me again by trading goalie Ed Belfour while still in his prime, and who would win a Stanley Cup two years later with the Dallas Stars. In 1999, the Hawks disgusted me by trading native Chicagoan and third key member Chris Chelios to the hated Detroit Red Wings, of all places. None of those guys wanted to leave Chicago, but now they were all gone.

Free-falling in the standings, a run of twenty-seven straight playoff appearances came to an end in 1998. The team made only one very short playoff appearance over the next eleven years. The Blackhawks were terrible and the fans left in droves. Routine sellouts now gave way to regular crowds of 5,000 in an arena that held 22,000. Like the DePaul Blue Demons a decade earlier, the Hawks slipped into oblivion and off Chicago's radar screen. My brother Dave, the biggest Hawk fan of the three of us, stopped watching them, and I tuned them, and hockey, out completely. I went over ten years without watching a Blackhawk game until my interest peaked for an outdoor hockey game on New Year's Day of 2009.

CHAPTER 15

One Goal

By 2007, I had lived in Florida for over a decade, but my love for the teams of my youth, other than the Blackhawks, had not diminished. Through the explosion of the information age of the last fifteen years, I'm still able to watch all the games on DirecTV. I read the sports sections online from both the *Chicago Tribune* and *Sun-Times* every morning and have 670 AM, "The Score," on over the Internet as background filler for a portion of my work day.

The Blackhawks completely dropped off the sports radar in Chicago—a decade of bad teams and bad front office decisions led to disgust within the fan base for ownership. Aside from poor attendance, the fans' tuning out the Hawks was evidenced by the sparse coverage in the media. I remember feeling sorry for the writers who covered the Hawks, and the only time a column was written it read more like an obituary bemoaning the fall of a once-proud franchise—one of the "Original Six" teams of the National Hockey League. All of that began to change when team owner Bill Wirtz passed away in September of 2007.

Taking over for his father, Arthur, Bill Wirtz ran the Hawks for forty-one years and went to his grave not seeing the Hawks hoist a Stanley Cup during his tenure. Like anybody else in a position of power, the final analysis of Wirtz would be extremely complex. By all accounts, he was a good family man and solid philanthropist. I benefited indirectly from the Wirtz Family through Blackhawk Charities which, in part, funded the wheelchair sports program at the Rehab Institute of Chicago since 1982. So much of my travel and training camps, including the Paralympic tryouts in 1996, were on the Blackhawks' dime. Regardless, the opinion is pretty universal that Wirtz's old-fashioned ownership mentality ran the Hawks into the ground for the last decade of his life. Wirtz's son Rocky took over the team after his father's death and instantly changed the culture of the organization and the hearts and minds of the Blackhawks' then dormant fan base.

Rocky Wirtz immediately set off a chain of events to improve both the image and on-ice play of the organization. He hired John McDonough, who hired Scotty Bowman as senior advisor and then Scotty's son Stan as assistant general manager. As a coach, Scotty Bowman won a record nine Stanley Cups, so if anybody could help the Hawks win their first Cup since 1961, Bowman would be the guy. From a marketing standpoint, Wirtz immediately lifted the decades-long ban on televising home games. Putting home games on TV was no small gesture with Hawks fans nor was the re-hiring of announcer Pat Foley. Foley left the Hawks after the 2006 season after—surprise, surprise—a dispute with Bill Wirtz. For most Hawk fans, losing the familiar voice of the Hawks had been the last straw with the elder Wirtz. Further, the Hawks brought back legends and Hall of Famers with distant or estranged relationships like Bobby Hull, Stan

Mikita, and Tony Esposito as team ambassadors. The organization created a marketing slogan of "One Goal."

On the ice, then general manager Dale Tallon began to put together a team with potential. They promoted young stars in the making, like eighteen-year-old Patrick Kane and twenty-year-old Jonathon Toews (pronounced "Taze") everywhere in Chicago as the faces of the organization. For the first time in a long time, the columns I started reading coming out of the Chicago newspapers about the Blackhawks read more like hope and opportunity than an obituary.

In early 2008, with the young Hawks showing some on-ice promise, former star Denis Savard, now the head coach, went on a rant in a press conference and I started becoming engaged once again as a Hawk fan. After a tough loss, Savard let everybody know that losing and mediocrity would no longer be tolerated. His "Commit to the Indian" outburst challenged the team to commit to the Blackhawk organization with the same level of passion that the organization was committing to them. The fans began to engage as well, with attendance picking up dramatically and the quality of the on-ice product improving as well. Although the 2007–08 squad missed the playoffs for the tenth time in eleven seasons, the team finished with its first winning record since 2002 and only the second since 1996 when I witnessed Jeremy Roenick play his last game with the Blackhawks.

Expectations were high going into the 2008–09 season. In a move that was controversial yet eventually proved the right decision, the Hawks relieved team legend Denis Savard of his coaching duties four games into the season and reassigned him within the organization while hiring the more experienced Joel Quenneville as head coach. Apparently, the National Hockey League expected big things from the Hawks as well. The NHL now plays one game a year outdoors on New Year's Day in an attempt to get back to hockey's frozen pond roots. The League announced before the season that the Hawks would host the elite team of the NHL, the defending Stanley Cup Champion Detroit Red Wings, in the prestigious Winter Classic at Wrigley Field. The Blackhawks went into the Winter Classic with a buzz just beginning to circulate again about the team as they trailed the 25–7–5 (Win–Loss–Tie) Red Wings with a 20–8–7 record— good enough for second place in the division.

For me, the Winter Classic marked the first hockey game I watched since attending Game 7 of the 2004 Stanley Cup Finals in Tampa. As much as anything, my curiosity lay with watching an outdoor hockey game in the dead of winter, in the city I grew up in, in a park where I spent numerous summer days, and with a hockey team that now drew my attention for the first time in a decade. Even though the young Hawks lost to the veteran Red Wings that afternoon, professional hockey once again took its place on the Chicago sporting landscape. The official rebirth and resurgence of the Chicago Blackhawks, in my world, happened on January 1, 2009, and, as my brother Dave would tell me on more than one occasion, all of it occurred because "one guy died."

I began to follow, study, and watch as much of the Blackhawks as possible. Emotionally, I started getting attached and bonding from the standpoint of a fan the way I did in the mid 1980s and again in the early to mid '90s. Where, a year prior, I wouldn't have known a Hawk player if he knocked on my door and introduced himself, I now started to know players like Jonathon Toews and Patrick Kane the same way I had known guys like Chris Chelios and Jeremy Roenick twenty years ago. The Hawks ended the 2008–09 season with the third-best record in the fifteen-team Western Conference, their best finish since 1992–93, and made the playoffs for only the second time since 1997. Once there, they continued their growth process by beating the more physical Calgary Flames and the more veteran Vancouver Canucks to advance to the NHL's Final Four, the conference finals—a place the Hawks hadn't been since 1995. There, they were put away 4 games to 1 by those hated Red Wings, falling short of the Stanley Cup Finals. The Wings were just older, wiser, and better. But the Hawks were coming and kept talking all summer about the lessons they learned, the experience they gained, and how hard they knew they needed to work to take the next step. They signed Marian Hossa, one of Detroit's best players, in the off season and simultaneously strengthened themselves while weakening the Red Wings. I had the same feeling about them that I had with the 1984 Bears the year before they won their first Super Bowl and the 1989–90 Bulls a season prior to their first NBA title. I knew the Hawks would hoist the Stanley Cup.

When the season started in October, I enjoyed the month-long "free view" on DIRECTV's Center Ice package. But as the month came to an end, the realization set in that I'd only be able to watch a few nationally telecast games by not living in the Chicago area. Knowing that I didn't want to miss out on what I was convinced would be a special season, I negotiated with

DIRECTV to give me the entire season of Center Ice for only one fourth of the retail cost of $172. So for $43 (the average single game ticket price), I had access to every Hawk game. The Hawks didn't disappoint anybody during the first three months, as they beat both conference rivals Detroit and San Jose four out of six games. After a dominating 5–2 road victory against the Boston Bruins on January 7, the Hawks stood at the top of the NHL with a 31–10–3 record. But seldom does a team go through an entire season without adversity. As such, the young Hawks were about to encounter enough challenges and adversity over the last three months of the season to either mold them into a championship-caliber team or break them into a talented yet mentally soft team that ultimately falls short and underachieves. In team sports, the latter is much more prevalent, as the road to a championship is littered throughout sports history with talented teams void of enough inner strength to win a championship.

Without being tested and having things relatively easy for them throughout the course of the season, the Hawks went to Minnesota to play the inferior Wild team. In a microcosm of their season to that point, they had a relatively easy time in taking a dominating 5–1 lead with about fourteen minutes to go in the game. They then dropped their guard, took their success for granted, and saw the Wild chip away at their lead 5–2, 5–3, 5–4. Taking advantage of a wobbly Hawks team's lacking aggressiveness, the attacking Wild tied the game 5–5 with just over a minute to go and finished off the beaten Hawks with an Overtime win. While the Hawks stopped attacking and the defense went to sleep in front of him, goalie Cristobal Huet failed to bail his team out when they needed a big save. And so really for the first time, whispers before the season regarding the Blackhawks' goaltending now became a larger point of discussion.

The Hawks played pretty mediocre hockey over the next month and half, again showing alarming lapses in focus and effort in back to back nationally televised home games in early March. On Sunday, March 7, the Hawks blew a 2–0 lead by allowing five straight second period goals, again with Huet unable to make a big save, in losing to those rival Red Wings. Again the following Sunday the Hawks took a big lead, 3–0, and again they fell apart, this time as the Washington Capitals scored three straight goals in the final period and an overtime goal to win 4–3. This time, rookie goalie Antti Niemi played the role as culprit in the team's collapse. Niemi was untested and unknown, but clearly Huet was done as the Hawks' starting goalie. Quenneville gave Niemi the job out of default. Of any position in any sport, a hockey goaltender is most directly responsible for his team's success or failure. No matter how talented your team, you can't hide your weakest link when it's your goaltender. That said, the rest of the team wasn't playing very well either. Star players Patrick Kane (USA), Jonathon Toews (Canada), Duncan Keith (Canada), Brent Seabrook (Canada), and Marian Hossa (Slovenia) all logged heavy minutes for their national teams at the Olympics the previous month. Whether fatigue from the Olympics played a role or not, the Hawks needed to come together, find their inner strength, and find it quickly. Between that ugly Minnesota loss and a March 30 loss against a bad St. Louis Blues team, the Hawks record was 15–12–3, not exactly the mark of a championship-caliber team.

To make matters worse, divisional foes like Detroit and Nashville closed what once seemed like an insurmountable Hawk lead, putting a division title in jeopardy. San Jose subsequently took control of the Western Conference with the best record that once looked like it would belong to the Hawks. With questions swirling around the team and Chicago sports radio beginning to talk about an early playoff collapse, the Hawks returned to Minnesota for the first time since early January.

Gathering themselves in much the same way as the 2005 White Sox when they were on the verge of collapse, the Hawks shut out Minnesota 4–0 and went on to win six of their last seven games. More importantly, Antti Niemi stabilized their weak link in the net, giving up only fourteen total goals in the last seven games while allowing one or fewer goals in three of those games. The Blackhawks stepped back and regained their composure. They also recaptured their confidence while developing a mental toughness and edge, important for a still-young team. In doing so, they held off Detroit and Nashville to win the division, earning the number two (of eight playoff seeds) in the conference behind San Jose as they, and all of Chicago, stood ready for the playoffs.

Although admittedly a bigger baseball and football fan than hockey, I firmly believe that the Stanley Cup is the most cherished of all championship trophies and the hardest to win in all of team sports. After making the playoffs as one of sixteen teams in a thirty-team league, the Cup winner has to win four separate best-of-seven game series over the span of almost two months. I've seen many championship team captains take possession and hoist the Cup after winning it. I remember seeing Mario Lemieux skating around the Chicago Stadium ice hoisting The Cup above his head after the Penguins beat the Hawks in 1992. But never between 1996 and 2008 did I think I'd see the Hawks jersey underneath a hoisted Stanley Cup in my lifetime. But I felt going into Game 1 of their first series against Nashville like I felt before the season started and after last season ended. I told both of my brothers to get ready to watch history unfold because the Hawks were going to win the Cup for the first time since 1961.

In a lot of ways, the Stanley Cup playoffs provide a microcosm of life. You don't always perform to the best of your ability while making mistakes, but you need to correct those mistakes to become a better person or performer. Likewise, the fortunate breaks don't always come your way, but when they do, you need to capitalize. Events typically do not unfold or go as expected; however you need to adapt, act, and respond accordingly to adversity by taking advantage of the opportunities that arise. And, more than in any other sport, the Stanley Cup playoffs mirror life as the most talented teams on paper aren't always the teams advancing through and ultimately winning the Cup. The teams advancing and the ultimate winner are the squads gelling together from individual parts into one functioning unit, those teams willing to pay the price, sacrificing and enduring while playing through injuries. In hockey, the team with the most mental and emotional toughness usually ends up carrying the Cup at the end of the playoff marathon.

Each game and each series includes enough subplots and "moments of truth" with players stepping up and responding to keep advancing or ultimately falling short. During the 2010 playoff run for the Blackhawks, each series had one game standing out as a defining moment. In the opening round, the seventh seeded Nashville Predators gave the Hawks all they could handle. Again, nothing is given to you or guaranteed in any sport, regardless of ability. Although the Hawks were the second seed, the history of the NHL Playoffs since 1994 tells us that the seventh seed beats the second seed in the first round fifty percent of the time.

With that backdrop, the series came back to Chicago tied 2–2 for Game 5. Game 6 would be in Nashville, so it became paramount for the Hawks to win Game 5 and avoid dropping down 3–2 in the series and then facing an elimination game on the road. The Hawks were not having their best game and found themselves down 4–3 with under a minute remaining. Further complicating matters, the Hawks played the final minute short-handed, five against six, as Marian Hossa sat in the penalty box after receiving a five-minute boarding penalty. Never had a team scored short-handed to tie a game in the last minute of an NHL playoff game—until now. With the Predators playing keep-away behind the Hawks net, they lost possession after an errant pass which the Hawks intercepted with about thirty seconds left. Racing up the ice came the Hawks while showing great composure with puck possession. Jonathon Toews took a shot from about fifteen feet out; the puck deflected and found the stick of Patrick Kane in front of the net who quickly rammed it in to somehow tie the game with only thirteen seconds left. The United Center crowd roared, bringing back memories of the old Stadium and giving the resilient Hawks a standing ovation with the game tied 4–4 going into overtime.

As the sudden death overtime began, however, the Hawks still needed to kill the remaining four minutes of Hossa's penalty. Playing five on six for four minutes is an eternity to keep an opposing team from scoring, but that's what the Hawks did as they fed off of the energy of the crowd. They out-skated Nashville to clear the puck of the zone every chance they had, laid down to block shots with any part of their body necessary, got a couple of big saves from Niemi, and, when defenseman Brent Sopel carried the puck into the Predator zone to kill the final seconds of the penalty, the Hawks were in business. After passing the puck around the boards, Sopel sent a shot that deflected right to Hossa, who shot the game winner into the net seconds after getting back on the ice from the penalty box. Marian Hossa and Patrick Kane, the team's most dangerous goal scorers, both put themselves in positions to capitalize on advantageous puck deflections to lead the team to victory. The Hawks were up 3–2 and the series was over two days later as the Hawks finished off Nashville in Game 6. More and more I started to sense that the Hawks were a team of destiny.

A second round rematch from the previous year took place with the Vancouver Canucks. The Canucks were a formidable opponent, having finished the regular season third in the conference behind San Jose and the Hawks. They dominated the Hawks for a Game 1 victory and quickly struck for two early goals in Game 2. Games 3 and 4 would be in Vancouver so the Hawks couldn't afford to fall down 2 games to 0. Once again gathering the necessary resolve, they battled back and tied the game at 2 with a short-handed goal by Patrick Sharp with about thirteen minutes left in the game. Kris Versteeg put in the game winner with a minute and a half to go as the Hawks took momentum in the series. Led by hat tricks (three goals in one game) by Dustin Byfuglien in Game 3 and Jonathon Toews in Game 4, they easily won both games in Vancouver, where they returned in Game 6 to win the series 4 games to 2.

A conference finals re-match with Detroit did not occur, however, as the number one seeded San Jose Sharks dominated the Wings 4 games to 1 in their series. Truth be told, most Hawk fans, myself included, will forever fear the Red Wings and were happy to get San Jose even though they'd have home ice advantage with Games 1, 2, 5, and 7. The Hawks played better during the playoffs to that point on the road than at home where they seemed to relax and lose their edge. So they went into Game 1 confident against a powerful Shark team fueled by a boisterous crowd. The first game provided the defining game of the series with the single defining moment coming later in Game 4. Game 1 was the game where any doubt or questions remaining about the Hawks were wiped away because goaltender Antti Niemi would have a Hall of Fame–worthy performance. Niemi stonewalled a furious onslaught by the Sharks in amassing forty-four saves as the Hawks held on for a 2–1 win. Five Hawks penalties, as opposed to zero by San Jose, led to ten minutes of power play, meaning the Hawks were short-handed for twenty percent of the game. Everybody thought if the Hawks were tough enough to win a game on the road while withstanding a hostile crowd and playing short-handed as much they did, they should be able to win the series. After taking Game 2 in San Jose, the Hawks returned home determined to remain focused and not let their guard down, as had been their previous pattern for the playoffs. Byfuglien's game winner in overtime of Game 3 reversed the trend; now up 3 games to 0, they looked to close out the Sharks and return to the Stanley Cup Finals for the first time since 1992.

Even with a 3–0 series lead, you never want to take anything for granted, especially after just witnessing a resilient team in Philadelphia coming back down 0–3 in their playoff run. San Jose is a powerful team capable of winning four in a row; so as a fan, I wanted to see the Hawks finish off San Jose, as opposed to giving them any reason for hope. The Sharks served notice early, with a determined effort indicating that they would not go down lightly. San Jose took a 1–0 lead into the second period when the defining play of the Hawks season and one that will be remembered throughout their history took place. On a power play, the Hawks were attempting to tie the game when the Sharks tried clearing the zone of the puck. The lifted puck hit Hawk defenseman Duncan Keith square in the mouth. As both he and seven of his teeth fell to the ice, a short-handed opportunity was created for the Sharks, who came down the ice with a man advantage, ultimately scoring and taking a 2–0 lead. Keith, after taking a few Novocain shots in the mouth, summoned the courage and determination necessary of a champion and returned to the ice, void of excuses, after missing only one shift. The moment energized the crowd as well as the Hawks who responded with two second period goals to send the game to the third period tied 2–2. When Byfuglien scored at the end of a power play with just under six minutes to go, the Hawks were on their way to the Finals. With the crowd standing and cheering, the Hawks played flawless possession hockey for the last five minutes of the game, not about to let the opportunity slip away. An empty netter in the final minute clinched the series sweep of the Sharks and put the Hawks four wins away from hoisting the Cup with their confidence in their individual and collective abilities at its peak.

Standing in the way would be the Philadelphia Flyers, a team with less talent but one of the most mentally tough teams in any sport in recent years. The Flyers had to win an overtime shootout in the last game of the regular season just to get into the playoffs. As the seventh seed in the Eastern Conference, they defeated the second seeded New Jersey Devils before falling behind 3 games to 0 in the conference semifinals to the Boston Bruins. Thirty-five years had passed since an NHL team last came back from a 0–3 deficit in a playoff series. But a combination of Philly's resilience and Boston's resting on their laurels allowed for the best comeback in a generation. The Flyers took advantage when an opportunity presented itself as, facing elimination in overtime, they beat Boston 5–4. They then won Games 5 and 6 to tie the series before finding themselves down 3–0 fifteen minutes into Game 7. But a belief began to build after Game 4 amongst the Flyer players and coaches in their collective ability to overcome any obstacle. They eventually tied the game, scored the go-ahead goal in the final period, and withstood a tenacious Bruin push in the final minutes to win the game 4–3 and the series 4–3.

Going into the Stanley Cup Finals, a consensus seeped into the Chicago sports psyche that the Hawks' time had arrived. The slogan of "One Goal" would be achieved. I knew the Hawks were the more talented team and if they could equal the dedication, determination, and effort of the Flyers—no easy task—then they'd win the Cup for the first time since 1961. The Hawks did equal the Flyers in their work ethic in winning Games 1 and 2, each by a single goal, and went to Philadelphia up 2 games to 0 and riding the momentum of a seven-game playoff winning streak and a 7–1 road record in the playoffs. The prevailing question within the Chicago media was whether or not the Hawks played their final home game of the season as many thought a sweep inevitable, predicting the Hawks would win games 3 and 4 in Philly. When Patrick Kane scored on a go-ahead breakaway goal to give the Hawks a 3–2 lead with seventeen minutes to go, the look and smell of a game winner that would put the Hawks up 3 games to 0 appeared. Well, apparently the Flyers didn't receive the email about the impending Hawks anointing. Twenty seconds later, Flyer playoff hero Ville Leino stunned the still celebrating Hawks while reviving a dormant crowd with the tying goal. The Hawks never recovered in Game 3, and after they suffered a mental lapse in overtime, the Flyers capitalized with the game winner and put themselves back in the series with a 4–3 win.

Picking up where they left off, the Flyers took advantage of some lapses and mistakes by the Hawks to win Game 3 as the series headed back to Chicago tied 2–2 for Game 5. After Friday night's loss, Saturday and Sunday were anxiety-ridden days leading up to Sunday night's game. Like the first round against Nashville, Game 5 was a must win as the Hawks couldn't go back to Philly facing an elimination game. With gloom and doom in the Chicago air, particularly among Cub fans, the discussion went from a Hawk sweep before Game 3 to a colossal collapse after Game 4. I even called my brother Dave asking him to reassure me that there was no way they could lose 4 out of 5 games. Dave was pretty confident they'd respond positively as they'd done all year long when faced with adversity. Flyer coach Peter Laviollete stayed busy in the media trying to gain the psychological edge. He strategically pointed out the pressure that the Hawks and, in particular, rookie goalie Antti Niemi had to be feeling trying to win a Cup for the first time in almost fifty years. With less mentally tough franchises like the Cubs, who have a way of always crumbling under the weight of their past, these tactics might have worked.

But the Blackhawks were not the Cubs. They came on the ice to another roar reminiscent of the old Stadium which, as always, continued right through the National Anthem, and the Hawks hit the ice flying at face-off. Quenneville changed up the Hawk lines. In particular, he split up the first line of Toews, Kane, and Byfuglien. Byfuglien responded with his best game. The Hawks were faster, hit harder, and showed they wanted it more in getting to loose pucks. The hard work paid off as they held a 3–0 lead at the end of the first period. Philly hung tough but never closed within two goals and with a 7–4 lead in the final minute, the last seconds ticked away with 22,000 fans on their feet chanting "We want the Cup! We want the Cup!" When the final horn sounded, the Hawks left the ice to a standing ovation while the Center Ice scoreboard showed a shiny Stanley Cup with the number 1 on it, signifying one more victory to win the most treasured trophy in all of sports.

With the Stanley Cup in the building, the Hawks took the ice with great anticipation for Game 6. Dominating the action early, the Hawks scored the all important first goal to go up 1–0. Their over-exuberance, though, also led to three first period penalties, and the Flyers finally capitalized with the man advantage on their third power play to tie the score 1–1 at the end of the first period. Philly went up 2–1 eight minutes into the second. But the unfazed Hawks always kept their eyes on the larger goal. Despite 20,000 rambunctious Philly fans, the Hawks never caved while tying it on a Patrick Sharp goal and then taking the lead on a shot by Andrew Ladd to go into the third period up 3–2. "Twenty minutes," read the text message I sent my dad and brothers—meaning the Hawks would be champions after twenty more minutes of play. For a while, that appeared to be the case as the minutes started dwindling away: ten minutes, eight minutes, six minutes, five minutes. But the Hawks had become a little too cautious with about fifteen minutes left, a long time to try to ice a one-goal lead against a tenacious team like Philadelphia. Sure enough, the "won't die" mentality of the Flyers kicked in as, with the Hawks but four minutes away from hoisting the Cup, Philly scored to tie the game.

The crowd went from silent to crazed and Blackhawk fans back in Chicago went from anticipation to panic. *We have to win this series now!* was the prevailing thought of the Hawks and their fans. Nobody wanted to go to a Game 7, as anything can happen and a championship can be won or lost on a fluke goal resulting from a weird bounce of the puck. From that point forward, I kept my finger on the off button on the remote, prepared to immediately turn the game off if the Flyers scored again. The Hawks went into the locker room at the end of regulation with the choice of feeling sorry for themselves while going over all the what-if scenarios or finding the strength and courage to come out and win it all right then in the sudden-death overtime. After withstanding a strong surge by Philadelphia early in the overtime, the time would come for a team to rewrite a franchise's recent wretched history and for a star to forever be a Chicago sports icon on the level of Payton and Jordan.

Four minutes into the overtime, Patrick Kane took a pass from Brian Campbell. Kane froze the defender with a shake and bake move, and as Kane skated in toward the net, he let loose a shot that literally would remain frozen in time for about five seconds before anybody realized the puck was stuck under the netting in the back of the net. The TV announcers were speechless, the referee didn't signal a goal, nor did the goal lamp light up. Michael Leighton, the Philly goaltender, sat helplessly still and the Philly defenders stood motionless, frozen numb, while Kane skated around the back of the net, throwing his helmet and his stick in the air the way a twelve-year-old does in his driveway as he fantasizes about scoring the game-winning goal. As he skated past the Blackhawk bench and the players poured onto the ice in jubilation, the reality hit every Hawk fan that it was over—all the suffering, pain, and misery gave way to peace, fulfillment, and joy.

For the Hawks, all the hard work, commitment, sacrifice, tough choices, endurance, and perseverance in the revival of the Chicago Blackhawk organization came to fruition as "One Goal" became reality. Minutes later, as the red carpet was laid out, two men in tuxedos and white gloves carefully brought the shiny Stanley Cup onto the ice. NHL commissioner Gary Bettman presented the Cup to twenty-two-year-old captain Jonathon

Toews, known as Captain Serious for his calm and professional demeanor. Toews let loose a "yeah baby!" howl as he hoisted the Cup above his head with two hands while my brother sent me a text that said "best jersey in all of sports"—a jersey with a logo nobody over the last decade thought they'd ever see hoisting that big, beautiful, shiny Cup.

For me, I appreciated "One Goal" because it brought me full circle as a fan in seeing guys I first came to know twenty-seven years ago, like Hawk legend Denis Savard and announcer Pat Foley, recognized by the organization at the victory celebration two days later. The parade down Michigan Avenue drew two million people cascaded in a sea of red to see a hockey franchise that couldn't draw 10,000 to a game four years earlier. I thought about all those games I attended with my brothers and all those heartbreaking losses. I cried as I watched Jeremy Roenick, now an NBC hockey analyst, cry during the post game wrap-up as he became emotional in saying, "This is really emotional for me … For the kid that was there in 1992 who was crying as I came off the ice after we lost Game 4 in Chicago Stadium, you waited eighteen years, I hope you have a big smile on your face … it's the Chicago Blackhawks, man. I never got to do that [hoist the Cup]. It's pretty unbelievable … I'm proud and happy."

In my almost thirty-five years as a diehard Chicago fan, I've seen the city go from a sports laughingstock in the late '70s and early '80s to, in a lot of ways, the city of champions. The arc of Chicago sports in that timeframe went from losing and despair when I first started following sports to a winning sports city. Every team, except one, figured out how to overcome years of mediocrity and disappointment. Chicago is the only city in the last thirty-five years to win championships in all four professional sports, and its nine champions are more than that of any other city within the last quarter century outside of New York—ten.

CONCLUDING THOUGHTS

For me, the true lasting memories from the Hawks' Stanley Cup run are enjoying the moments with my four-year-old Nico while beginning to instill the value of sport and competition in him. Too young to stay up and watch the games live, he often asked to watch "the sports show" with me, so we watched the key moments recorded on DVR—the Kane winner, the celebration, the parade. I have a puck given to me at a game in 1991 that sat on display in my home office. Nico now insists he needs the "Backhawk puck" for his "office" and displays the puck on his bedroom dresser next to his Bears helmet. Setting up a hockey rink on the tile floor in our living room, Nico's imagination ran wild as he grabbed a large plastic bin for a goal and brooms and a rubber ball for us to play "hawkey." Of course, he always wins and has me make the sound of the now commonplace goal horn first heard at the old Chicago Stadium after all his goals.

Nico refers to the Stanley Cup as the "big trophy," and in his four-year-old mind, the Blackhawks are the only team to win the Cup. Days later we went to Sports Clips here in Tampa to get his haircut and he pointed, saying "look, the big trophy" while pointing to a poster of the 2004 champion Tampa Bay Lightning. He asked, "Where da backhawks?" to which I tried explaining how different teams win in different years and you can't keep the

Cup forever. But he was having none of my explanation because as far as he's concerned, that's the "backhawk's big trophy" and nobody else's. And so it goes as a seed is planted with the next generation and a bond is strengthened with a common memory between father and son.

My childhood was an era in which youth participation in team sports as well as following your closest city's professional teams were commonplace and expected. Especially with baseball, and in some cases football, every boy in my neighborhood at one point played organized ball. The baseball field down my street always filled up with pick-up games in the summer and, in football season, a two-hand touch game went on somewhere on my street. All of this, for a variety of reasons, has dissipated in our current culture. Empirical evidence and most studies indicate that interest in sports by kids and that youth participation in team sports are down significantly over the last twenty-five years. As a result, the fabric of sporting interests unifying communities through civic pride no longer is the norm. The shared sense of a community of parents, neighborhoods, and kids coming together through participation in team sports has dwindled significantly over the past thirty years. Our disjointed or inward society of today stunts the potential of many in our youth culture.

That foundation as well as the encouragement, support, and common bond within my family greatly shaped and influenced the path I've taken since that fateful day in June of 1989 when a bullet ripped through my neck. I hope to impart my experiences and knowledge to my children. Nico, like any typical four-year-old, asks a thousand mundane questions but only recently asked why I can't walk. Very casually one day as we sat watching his favorite cartoon, he asked out of nowhere:

"Dada, why do you use a wheel-da-chair?"

"Because my legs don't work," I said.

Nico replied, "What for?"

"Because when I was a little boy, I didn't listen to my mommy or daddy," I answered, planting a seed to teach him a valuable life lesson.

By using teachable moments from my own life and the games I watch, as well as from the teams I follow, I'll look to teach my children to stay on the right course, to win with grace, and to lose with dignity. I'll encourage their individual talents and personalities while molding them within the parameters and rules of our family unit. I'll show them how to play their various roles in their personal and professional relationships. I'll instruct them to accept responsibility, to be accountable, to learn effective ways of communication, and to properly correct their mistakes. Through my example, I pray they'll learn to take advantage of second chances and seize opportunities while training, persevering, enduring, and overcoming daunting obstacles, while developing inner toughness along the way. All in all, I pray every day that my children will fulfill all the potential and promise instilled in them by the Lord.

ABOUT THE AUTHOR

G rowing up in the suburbs of Chicago, Bill was shot in neck and permanently paralyzed as a 17-year-old in 1989. From there, he set out on a path of endurance and perseverance ultimately earning a B.A and M.S in Journalism from the University of Illinois. He was a three-time member of Team USA wheelchair rugby winning Gold in the 1996 Atlanta Paralympics, the 1998 World Championships in Toronto and the 2000 Sydney Paralympics. Since 2002, Bill has been an award-winning commercial real estate broker in the Tampa Bay Area. With Amy, his lovely wife of 10 years, and their three children, Bill lives in Wesley Chapel, FL where he and Amy have been actively-involved members of Idlewild Baptist Church for over a decade.

VISIT BILL RENJE AT HIS WEBSITE:
www.achosenbullet.com